DEVELOPMENT IN PRACTICE

East Asia's Trade and Investment

East Asia's Trade and Investment

Regional and Global Gains from Liberalization

THE WORLD BANK
WASHINGTON, D.C.

The Development in Practice series publishes reviews of the World
Bank's activities in different regions and sectors. It lays particular emphasis on the progress that is being made and on the policies and practices
that hold the most promise of success in the effort to reduce poverty in the
developing world.

This report is a study by the World Bank's staff, and the judgments made
herein do not necessarily reflect the views of the Board of Executive
Directors or of the governments they represent.

The boundaries, colors, denominations, and other information shown on
the map in this volume do not imply on the part of the World Bank Group
any judgment on the legal status of any territory or the endorsement or acceptance of such boundaries.

ISBN 0-8213-2959-6

A year ago, the publication *Sustaining Rapid Development in East Asia and the Pacific* (World Bank 1993d) identified several issues as major challenges facing the region. As a followup, the present report looks in some depth at one of these issues—namely, trade and investment reforms.

This report, prepared by the Office of the Vice President, East Asia and Pacific Region, is based on economic and operational work in the region and other parts of the World Bank. The principal authors were Ramgopal Agarwala, Peter Petri, and Vinod Thomas. Important contributions were made by Paul Armington, Carlos Braga, Thomas Chan, Hoon Mok Chung, Michael Finger, Jeffrey Hammer, Nobuko Ichikawa, Osamu Kawaguchi, Kali Kondury, Will Martin, Ashoka Mody, Arvind Panagariya, Anthony Rowley, John Shilling, T. G. Srinivasan, Peter Stephens, Yan Wang, Koji Yanagishima, and Alexander Yeats. The report was produced under the general guidance of Gautam Kaji.

Many people inside and outside the Bank provided valuable comments and contributions. Data from the World Bank's International Economics Department were the basis for the analytical parts of the report. The support staff of the report included Carmencita Clay, Okie Moon Dorian, Amara Gumnerdngam, and Jae Shin Yang. Bruce Ross-Larson was the principal editor; Kathryn Kline Dahl copyedited the final manuscript and coordinated publication.

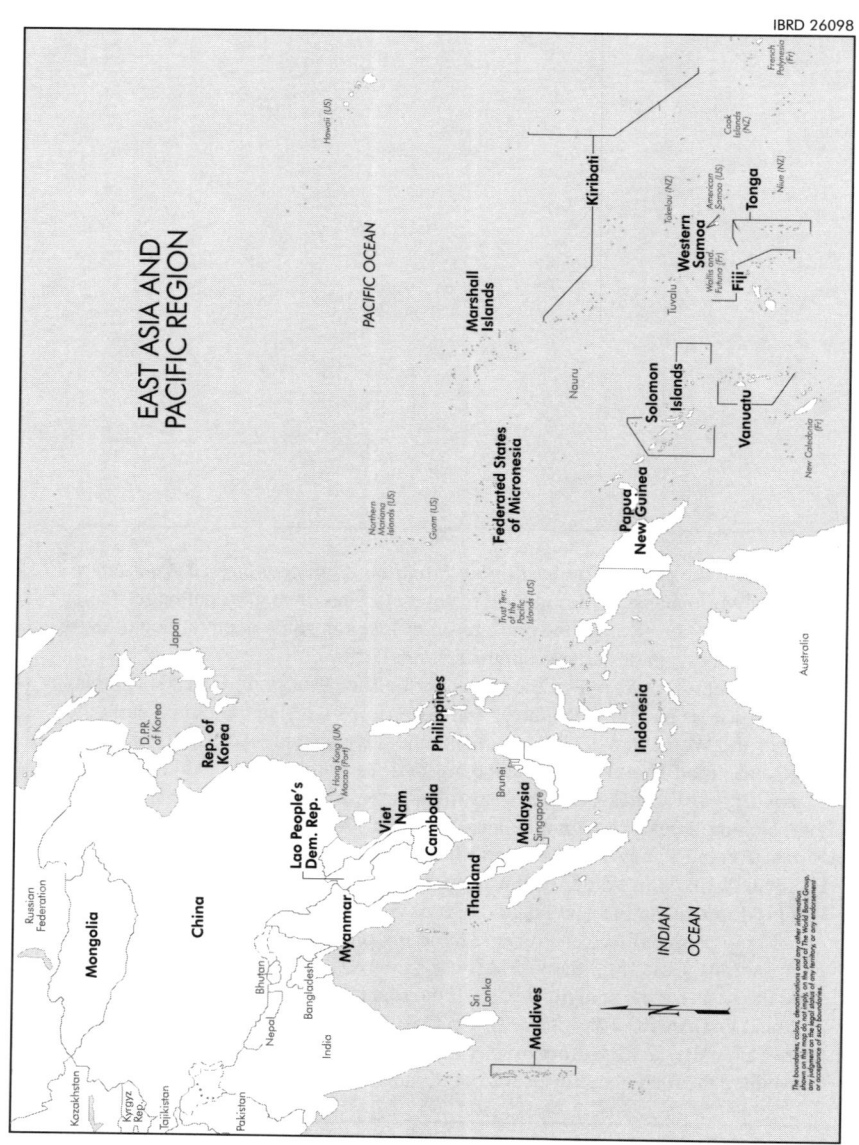

EAST ASIA AND PACIFIC REGION

Contents

Boxes

Figures

Text tables

Appendix tables

Foreword

INTERNATIONAL trade is the foundation of East Asia's impressive economic growth. The completion of the Uruguay Round of global trade talks was, therefore, an event of great significance and promise for East Asia—just as the trade tensions that marked prior years loomed large as a threat to the region's continued prosperity. Now is an opportune moment for taking additional, preemptive steps toward multilateral trade liberalization—and away from protection and inward-looking regionalism.

East Asia is well placed to initiate more liberal trade and investment:

- Sustained rapid growth makes East Asia a major player in global trade and investment.
- The region's large trade surpluses are not economically and politically sustainable.
- Despite considerable progress, East Asia still has substantial trade barriers that can be reduced.
- The additional trade liberalization can be financed by foreign direct investment. And simultaneously freeing trade and investment will allow more efficient technology transfers.

A regionwide approach could have a larger scope and larger benefits than unilateral measures alone, provided that protective barriers against imports from all countries around the world were lowered on a nondiscriminatory basis. This approach could bring additional gains equal to about one-half of the global gains envisaged under the Uruguay Round, with especially large dividends for East Asia. Benefits to the rest of the world are substantial, too, through increased openings for trade and investment.

The economic arguments for continuing liberalization are compelling, but they leave unanswered the pivotal question of how such a process would survive politically. One lesson from the seven years of Uruguay Round negotiations is that trade reform cannot continue without broad political support. On this score, there is reason for optimism in East Asia because governments in the region have shown themselves time and again to be unusually pragmatic and willing to make tough decisions in the national interest. East Asia now has a chance both to lead and to benefit—an opportunity that it should seize eagerly. Equally, industrial countries could support this approach by refraining from unilateralism and inward-looking regionalism and by promoting freer global trade and investment.

An important first step in building a consensus on this issue is to disseminate evidence of the potential economic gains from freer trade and investment. This report provides such evidence, and it is my sincere hope that it will form the basis for discussion and consideration among the East Asian countries. The World Bank will be happy to support such a dialogue within the region.

Gautam S. Kaji
Regional Vice President
East Asia and Pacific Region

Acronyms and Data Note

AFTA	ASEAN Free Trade Area
APEC	Asia-Pacific Economic Cooperation
ASEAN	Association of Southeast Asian Nations
EAEG	East Asian Economic Group
EU	European Union
FDI	Foreign direct investment
GATT	General Agreement on Tariffs and Trade
GDP	Gross domestic product
MFA	Multifiber arrangement
MFN	Most favored nation
MITI	Ministry of International Trade and Industry (Japan)
NAFTA	North American Free Trade Agreement
NIES	Newly industrializing economies
SITC	Standard International Trade Classification
OECD	Organization for Economic Cooperation and Development

Note: Dollars ($) are U.S. dollars throughout.

Executive Summary

EAST Asia is well placed to spark further liberalization of global trade and investment, in a role analogous to that played by the United States and Europe following World War II.[1] Unilateral liberalization remains beneficial, but concerted action promises a broader liberalization and greater benefits than do unilateral efforts alone. Concerted action does *not,* however, mean the formation of a preferential or discriminatory bloc. Indeed, a regional initiative would be especially beneficial to the region and the world if it were nondiscriminatory—that is, based on the most-favored-nation (MFN) principle rather than on preferential arrangements. Integrating liberalization of foreign direct investment (FDI) into this process—supported by additional investments from industrial countries—could make trade reforms much bolder and more productive.

An Unprecedented Opportunity

In November 1993 the U.S. Congress approved the North American Free Trade Agreement (NAFTA), clearing the way for its implementation on January 1, 1994. Also in November, the leaders of the Asia-Pacific Economic Cooperation (APEC) met for the first time to discuss trade and FDI policy reforms in the region. Leaders of the Association of Southeast Asian Nations (ASEAN) continued to deliberate steps toward an ASEAN free trade area.[2] In December the Uruguay Round of the General Agreement on Tariffs and Trade (GATT) ended with an agreement for substantial liberalization of global trade. And reflecting the GATT's enlarged areas of activity, a new world trade organization is being created.

All this is good news for open trade, both regional and global. There had been fears that regionalism would triumph over multilateralism, an outcome that would have been costly for developing countries. The conclusion of the Uruguay Round is important not only for the tangible trade liberalization it promises but also for the signal that further gains can now be made within a strong framework of multilateralism.

There is no cause for euphoria, however. Difficult negotiations remain in working out the details of the Uruguay Round agreements and in implementing the results. Also, the global economic recovery is likely to remain slow for some time. East Asia's trade surpluses continue to be large, and they are economically and politically unsustainable in the global setting. And for many developing East Asian countries, protection rates are higher than they were in the industrial countries at the beginning of the GATT rounds, though they have come down considerably in most countries over the past ten years. So the potential for trade tensions and protectionism remains serious—unless the progress under the Uruguay Round is reinforced by further action.

The world trading system needs a locomotive to maintain its momentum toward greater openness, and East Asia, in view of its rapid economic growth, is well positioned to provide leadership. The case is strengthened by the expectation that this region's exports will gain more than others from the Uruguay Round agreement. In purchasing power parity terms, the region now accounts for about 25 percent of global output. Japan and developing East Asia combined are projected to account for some two-fifths of new purchasing power during 1992–2000 and one-third to one-half of new imports (figure 1). A major trade liberalization in East Asia would thus provide enormous gains—not only to the region but also to the rest of the world. The industrial countries would do well to encourage such liberalization by turning away from threats of inward-looking regionalism, aggressive trade retaliation, and indirect protection.

A Changing External Environment

Over the past quarter century, East Asia's exports rose more than thirtyfold to about $850 billion, raising East Asia's share of world exports from about 7 percent to 21 percent. This rapid increase in market penetration could not have occurred without a supportive international environment—including steady reductions in trade barriers in the United States and other industrial countries orchestrated under the GATT. But as East Asia's trade surpluses mounted (figure 2) and as growth slowed among members of the Organization for Economic Cooperation and Development (OECD), the postwar trading system came under stress, suggesting that such large surpluses are not politically sustainable in the long term.

Some countries with trade deficits developed regulatory practices ostensibly to prevent dumping, a move that created uncertainty for all export-oriented

During the rest of this decade, East Asia is likely to account for at least a third of new imports.

FIGURE 1   REGIONAL SHARES OF THE INCREASE IN IMPORTS, 1992–2000

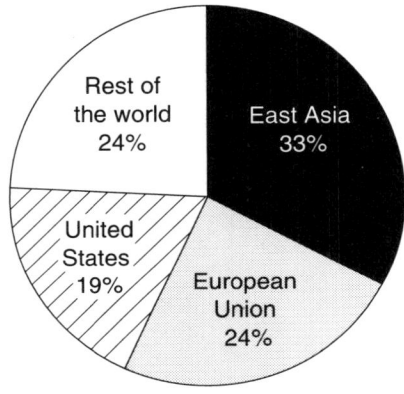

Note: Based on conservative estimates for East Asia.
Source: IMF *Direction of Trade Statistics* (various issues); World Bank staff estimates.

strategies. Some negotiated voluntary export restraints to bypass GATT restrictions on quotas. And some adopted legislation that required retaliation against any country believed to be practicing unfair trade. Often these interventions were directed against developing and newly industrializing economies (NIEs). The Uruguay Round of GATT negotiations sought to curb these practices as well as extend the coverage of the GATT to new areas. The implementation of the Uruguay Round is expected to reduce tariffs and some quantitative restrictions and, as a result, add about 1 percent to the global gross domestic product (GDP) over ten years. The Uruguay Round also succeeded in extending the GATT to some new areas and led to the efforts now under way to establish a new world trade organization that will supersede the mandate of the GATT.

Rapid movements of capital, information, and technology have narrowed the gap between real wages and interest rates in industrial and in newly industrializing economies. While the early postwar trading system provided developing countries more favorable treatment in the GATT, the environment today is less tolerant of such special treatment. Industrial countries are reluctant to offer continued access to their own markets—where East Asian imports have recently grown 15 to 20 percent a year—without gaining better access to

East Asia's growing trade surpluses might be unsustainable over the long term.

FIGURE 2   EAST ASIA'S TRADE SURPLUSES WITH THE UNITED STATES
AND THE EUROPEAN UNION

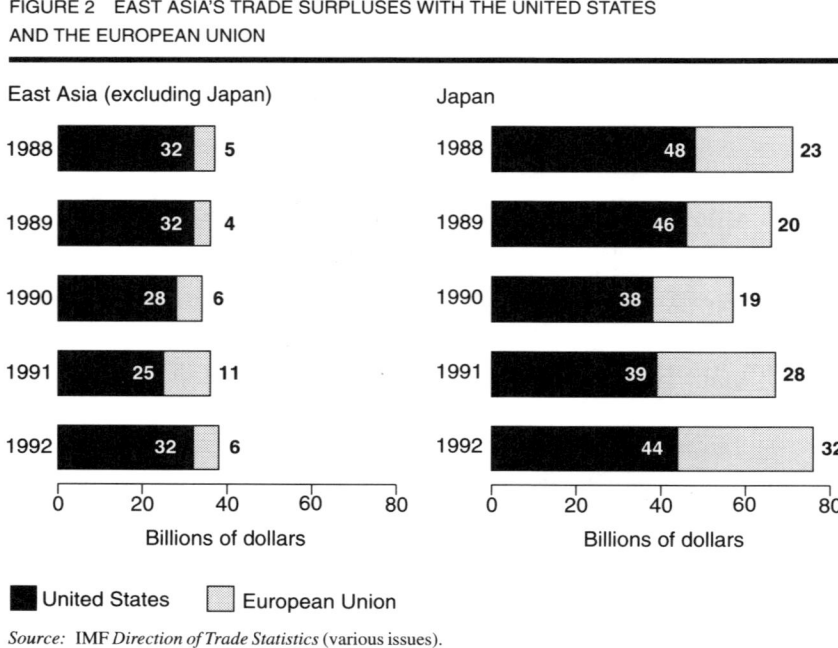

East Asia (excluding Japan)   Japan

1988   32   5   1988   48   23
1989   32   4   1989   46   20
1990   28   6   1990   38   19
1991   25   11   1991   39   28
1992   32   6   1992   44   32

   0   20   40   60   80   0   20   40   60   80
        Billions of dollars   Billions of dollars

■ United States   □ European Union

Source: IMF *Direction of Trade Statistics* (various issues).

developing-country markets. Unresolved, these differences could lead to further tensions in the world trading system. Already at the beginning of 1994 there were signs of political and trade conflicts between the United States on the one hand and Japan and China on the other.

Trade wars can do enormous damage, as the 1930s showed, and as indicated by low-case scenarios of downside global developments. The completion of the Uruguay Round provides an opportunity to restore the foundations of multilateralism by new and innovative extensions of the GATT philosophy.

East Asia's Economic Integration

Over the years, the East Asian economies have become increasingly important to each other. Strong links also developed between East Asia and the rest of the Pacific region. There have been a number of bilateral agreements (for example, between China and Japan, and between the United States and Singapore) and some regional initiatives (for example, ASEAN and the proposed East Asian Economic Caucus). East Asia's intraregional share of trade increased from about 33 percent in 1980 to 41 percent in 1992. Even so, that marks only a return to pre–World War II levels, and it is still less than the level of trade within Europe. Lowering barriers further within the region can thus bring benefits, allowing the region to take better advantage of geographic ties, production complementarities, and horizontal and vertical linkages.

The global economy witnessed a substantial slowdown in growth in the early 1990s. East Asia was the only region that was able to maintain very high growth rates during this time. One reason for this strong performance was the sharp increase in trade and investment within the region itself. The region's own markets are therefore critical to the sustainability of its growth.

There are limits, however, to intraregional expansion, and trade and output growth still depend on extraregional markets. In 1993 the region's export growth slowed to about one-half of the growth in 1992, partly in response to the economic slowdown outside the region. Indeed, East Asian ties to North America and Europe remain very important. Because more than half of the region's trade still depends on extraregional markets, East Asia needs a regional strategy, complementing country strategies, to encourage openness within East Asia, within the Pacific region, and with Europe and the rest of the world.

Trade Reform in East Asia

East Asia achieved dramatic progress through outward-oriented policies implemented within a global framework of increasing openness. The East Asian economies, including China and other socialist economies in transition, have been dropping protection levels and barriers to trade as well as to investments. This liberalization has boosted growth rates further and contributed enormously to lifting living standards.

But many developing countries in East Asia, as elsewhere, still have varying but substantial degrees of effective protection—for example, for manufacturing in China, Indonesia, the Philippines, Thailand, and Viet Nam. For several countries in the region, average effective protection rates in manufacturing have been 40 percent or more in recent years, higher than those that prevailed in industrial countries in the postwar period and at the beginning of the GATT rounds. There also are informal, quantitative restrictions to trade and investment (procurement practices, standards, administrative guidance) in the developing and industrial economies of East Asia.

The promised benefits that motivated liberalization in the past are greater today because of the expanded role of FDI (see below). In this connection, import protection is no longer justified by the old infant-industry arguments:

many of the protected industries are no longer infants, and much of the protection is costly. Some of the most spectacular recent stories of East Asian development—in Malaysia, for instance—have been led by FDI from Japan and the NIEs. These successes showed that the joint liberalization of trade and investment flows can provide a much more powerful boost to development than can import protection.

East Asia could substantially enhance its already impressive performance by launching a bold liberalization drive. This would involve rolling back both formal and informal barriers in the developing as well as the more industrial countries of East Asia. The reforms would vary across countries but would, on average, go well beyond the Uruguay Round agreements. Coupled with the positive role of the state in developing human resources, expanding infrastructure, and protecting the environment, such liberalization of trade could continue to produce handsome payoffs.

Reform of Investment Regimes

There has been a major shift in recent years in the role of FDI in development. New communication technologies and more competitive international markets are causing large firms to distribute their activities more aggressively across countries. Rather than establishing subsidiaries to exploit local markets (import-substituting FDI), multinationals are now adopting global strategies to link subsidiaries through global assembly and marketing networks in "borderless factories" (export-oriented FDI). In this context, infant-industry protection is counterproductive, since borderless factories require unrestricted flows of inputs and capital goods. In short, FDI is a more efficient instrument than import protection for developing new industries. Today, the simultaneous liberalization of trade and investment can help to promote international integration and technical progress.

East Asian economies have been attracting increasing amounts of FDI because of sound macroeconomic policies and an open investment climate. But further actions, varying across countries, can help in a number of areas. According to the evidence, such special FDI incentives as tax concessions and tax holidays are not necessary and may even be self-defeating. There is no defensible rationale for attracting FDI under protective walls for imports. The actions needed for relaxing FDI restrictions—regarding ownership, sectoral criteria, local content, and export obligations—differ from country to country. Some need to liberalize trade policies, and several need to liberalize capital flows further. Most countries will need to make more progress in deregulating labor markets and credit policies and in developing human resources and infrastructure and protecting the environment. Also crucial in many instances is the establishment of transparent regulatory and legal frameworks, which influence the quality of FDI.

Effective FDI flows also depend on policies—regarding taxes, for example—in the source countries. Japan has adopted several measures—in taxation, finance, and investment guarantees—to support Japanese investment abroad. Policies for technology transfers, good labor relations, the development of human resources, and the protection of the environment are also crucial for both the source and the recipient countries.

Options for Trade and Investment Liberalization

Given its stake in global multilateralism, East Asia will benefit by taking an active role in shaping the world trading system. Discussed below are options for liberalization, which are not mutually exclusive.

Liberalization on a Most-Favored-Nation Basis

Unilateral action. Traditionally, East Asian countries have liberalized unilaterally. Each of the region's economies has reduced impediments to trade and investment, in some cases gradually over time and in others in rapid bursts of reform. The process of liberalization has played an important role in the region's growth and is likely to continue doing so in the future.

The arguments for liberalization are, if anything, growing stronger. By opening their economies, countries gain access to more affordable consumer goods and to technologies and intermediate goods that help reduce production costs. Thus, by improving the climate for investment, liberalization also helps to attract foreign capital. Foreign investment, in turn, can provide the technology and financing required to establish a more efficient production structure.

Concerted MFN liberalization. Benefits are amplified and accelerated if the region's economies join in a policy of liberalization. Because each country gains from greater access to the markets of its regional partners, each can open its own markets more boldly without risking serious adjustment problems. This approach conforms strictly to the GATT and strengthens global liberalization. It combines two elements: regional action going beyond unilateral action, and liberalization on a most-favored-nation basis rather than discriminatory liberalization.

Regional liberalization offers great gains to East Asia itself—from lower production costs and lower costs of consumer goods to productivity gains (especially in manufacturing) and increased opportunities for specialization and investment. An open trading regime also promotes investments that help to finance the trade liberalization. An MFN approach to reducing remaining restrictions on imports and investments will benefit the rest of the world, especially East Asia's key trading and investment partners: Australia, Europe, and North America. The gains to partners will be greater if they too liberalize on an MFN basis. All this benefits the world trading system as a whole, making the region's growth more sustainable politically and economically.

Regional action on trade and investment will also provide a context for tackling other issues in East Asian economic integration. Environmental protection is an urgent regionwide priority, and countries will face lower risks of economic dislocation if they coordinate their strategies. Some types of environmental policies and investments, as well as such undertakings as infrastructure investments and safety standards, will benefit from regional coordination and could receive vigorous support from OECD partners in the context of a major regional initiative.

Preferential Liberalization

Whether unilateral or concerted, MFN approaches to trade and investment issues offer advantages over preferential arrangements. Discriminatory trading blocs among developing countries have often failed because they involve economies that have similar production advantages and disadvantages and limited possibilities for intraindustry trade. Consequently, most such blocs have had little impact on intrabloc trade, and some have even diverted imports from low-cost third-country sources to high-cost producers within the bloc.

Small, preferential, subregional blocs.   Under the ASEAN Free Trade Area (AFTA), trade restrictions among the six ASEAN countries—but not for other trading partners—would be largely eliminated in the next seven to fifteen years. This move could attract some additional foreign investment into ASEAN and streamline inefficient industries in some of its members. But unless global trade and investment barriers in these countries are reduced, this approach might have modest effects, including in some instances possible trade diversion from the rest of the world.

A large free trade area.   A large free trade area incorporating all East Asian countries could produce stronger results because of its size and the implied economies of scale. But a preferential or free trade area would be difficult to negotiate and could possibly divert East Asia's global trade patterns. Countries outside the region, including South Asia, would find it more difficult to link their economies to this dynamic area.

A Proposed Approach

Much of the political discussion on liberalization has centered on the costs of liberalization—and hence on the need for reciprocity. Concerted MFN liberalization makes a powerful case for the benefits of liberalization, especially when several countries jointly liberalize in a nondiscriminatory way. Developing-country experience with discriminatory trading blocs has been dismal. Equally unproductive would be discriminatory practices by industrial countries such as proposals for managed trade policies.

In light of these considerations, it would be useful for East Asian countries to explore a collective approach to liberalizing trade and investment over the next several years. The objective would not be to negotiate exact trade policies across countries but rather to confirm a common, nondiscriminatory approach and frameworks for action that complement country actions. The approach could aim for:

- A reduction in tariffs and in the tariff equivalent of quantitative restrictions by, say, 50 percent from the current levels in East Asian countries. This would go beyond the agreements reached under the Uruguay Round.
- Liberalization of FDI policies and mobilization of FDI in developing East Asia and the investor countries in both East Asia and the rest of the world. These actions together are expected to contribute to a doubling of FDI from the base levels.
- Cooperation on the critical issue of environmental protection as well as on other issues that affect trade and economic integration, such as infrastructure.

To facilitate the adoption of such a program by East Asia, the OECD countries need to reform their policies, thereby signaling strong support for MFN-type liberalization. And the multilateral agencies need to play a supportive role.

- The OECD countries need to eschew unilateralism, bilateral friction, and inward-looking regionalism and commit themselves to nondiscriminatory MFN approaches in trade and investment.
- Multilateral agencies would support developing East Asia in reforming policies and in augmenting FDI flows, beginning with more detailed discussions of the present proposal.
- The OECD countries and multilateral agencies could provide technical advice and financing to deal with the environmental and infrastructure implications of East Asia's integration initiatives.

Current World Bank projections of a base case for growth in GDP for the next decade suggest continued strong performance by East Asia. The base case assumes that policy reforms in the region are sustained and deepened. The base also envisages implementation of the Uruguay Round agreements, amounting to about a 30 percent tariff reduction in the OECD countries, as well as the binding of the unilateral tariff reductions already achieved, plus further tariff reductions of another 10–20 percent in the developing countries. All this implies substantial progress in the base case itself, which cannot be taken for granted but requires serious implementation.

The quantitative analysis in this report shows that substantial additional benefits in output and trade, above and beyond the base case, can be realized from further actions. In one analysis of the comparative static welfare gains, the global increase in income over a base level is estimated to be around 0.4 percent, or more than $100 billion above the level for year 2000, which is about half of the estimated gains from the Uruguay Round. The major beneficiaries would be China and ASEAN, followed by the NIEs and Japan. Australia, the European Union, the United States, and others would also gain, but not as much.

So the bulk of benefits from a regionwide liberalization would go to the region. East Asian countries would reap the productivity and cost reduction benefits of liberalization, as well as the benefits of trade augmentation. Developing East Asia would incur an additional trade deficit compared to the base case, but that would be broadly financed by increased investment flowing from reforms of investment regimes. The overall balance-of-payments effect would be to lower East Asia's trade surpluses and the deficits of the European Union and the United States, which would contribute to the political and economic sustainability of East Asia's outward-oriented strategy. The program would also increase the exports of the European Union and the United States, which should encourage them to support the initiative by refraining from unilateralism and inward-looking regionalism. They are also likely to benefit as a result of greater investments in East Asia. And if an MFN-type liberalization were extended in other regions, they would benefit even more.

Putting the initiative into a macroeconomic model of world growth shows similar benefits, in terms of deviations from a baseline growth rate. Trade liberalization together with related investment increases is shown to boost output by 0.4 percent a year from a base case around year 2000. The gains to East Asia and to other regions would be similar to those projected in the previous analysis.

In an alternative scenario, a reversal of some of the trade and investment liberalization could lower the growth rate by 0.8 percent a year. The global outlook is very uncertain. But the present proposal would tend to create a favorable global policy climate that will raise the probability of the upside opportunities and lower the probability of the downside risks. The estimate of a 0.8

percent decline in the growth rate in the downside scenario suggests that even a small reduction in the probability of such impairment in growth could translate into substantial benefits over time.

Conclusion

East Asia is well positioned to initiate further liberalization of global trade and investment, not only because it still retains substantial trade barriers and enjoys major trade surpluses but also because its economic dynamism will allow it to make relatively painless adjustments. Such an initiative would contribute significantly to the region's own welfare while also enabling it to absorb more exports from outside, thereby helping to defuse international trade tensions—provided that others respond in a nondiscriminatory way. For East Asia's major trading partners, supporting an initiative that creates new demand in a region already poised to absorb the largest share of incremental world imports must be more appealing than seeking to gain shares of existing markets in East Asia through far less dynamic (and more confrontational) approaches.

A regional initiative would benefit East Asia more if it were non-discriminatory and if benefits were offered on an MFN basis to all trading partners. The political benefit derived from the approach would be an added bonus. In this case the overall welfare gains—in trade, output, and productivity—would accrue in large measure to the region itself. But other countries would also gain from the increased opportunities for trade and investments. And the probability of an East Asian liberalization would be larger, and the gains to others would be greater, if they, too, were to liberalize further on an MFN basis.

CHAPTER ONE

A Changing External Environment

INTERNATIONAL trade and investment have been crucial to East Asia's outstanding development record. An export orientation and increasingly open markets overseas played a part in the so-called East Asian miracle (World Bank 1993a; Leipziger and Thomas 1993). The early exporters—Japan, Korea, and Taiwan (China)—adopted an export-push strategy with restrictions on imports and foreign direct investment, a strategy that worked in part because of the relatively open markets in the United States. The later exporters—Malaysia, Thailand, and the southern provinces of China—opted for an FDI-led strategy with increasingly liberal trade regimes. In today's trade environment, the mercantilist approach of the early exporters has lost favor. The new strategy clearly is more effective internationally and less costly in social terms.

Over time, East Asian trade has become increasingly large relative to the world's total. Meanwhile, the slowdown in OECD growth, coupled with large East Asian trade surpluses, has contributed to political and economic friction. The Uruguay Round agreement of the General Agreement on Tariffs and Trade will help to reduce some of these frictions, but it may not be enough. The completion of the Uruguay Round also signals the end of some of the special concessions. Clearly, more action on trade and investment liberalization in East Asia is warranted.

Global and Regional Economic Growth

The world economy has been sluggish, and global growth was modest in 1993. With recession in the OECD countries and the collapse of output in Eastern Europe and the former Soviet Union, global per capita output declined in 1991 for the first time since 1982—by around 1 percent (table 1.1). The decline, though smaller, continued in 1992 and in 1993. Some growth in output is expected in 1994, but the recovery is likely to be less robust than in the recovery years of 1976, 1984, and 1988.

Behind the OECD's weak performance are the halting recovery in the United States and the slowdowns in Europe and Japan. Despite lower interest rates, recovery has been slow in the United States. Europe's situation has been fragile, with volatile foreign exchange markets and interest rates. And the plunge in Japanese stock prices is but one aspect of the difficulties there. These short-term developments reinforce the long-term decline in productivity growth in industrial countries (figure 1.1). Furthermore, in all developing regions outside Asia, productivity growth was slower in the 1980s than in the 1970s.

Global per capita output declined in 1991 for the first time in a decade, and recovery has been sluggish.

TABLE 1.1   GROWTH OF GDP AND PER CAPITA GDP IN OECD AND DEVELOPING COUNTRIES

Indicator	1981–90 (annual average)	1991	1992	1993 (est.)	1994 (est.)
GDP					
World	2.9	0.7	1.3	1.3	2.2
Seven major OECD countries[a]	2.9	0.8	1.7	1.1	2.1
Low- and middle-income countries	3.0	0.3	−0.3	2.0	3.0
Excluding the former Soviet Union	3.0	2.4	3.6	4.3	4.3
GDP per capita					
World	1.1	−1.0	−0.3	−0.4	0.6
Seven major OECD countries[a]	2.2	0.2	1.2	0.6	1.5
Low- and middle-income countries	1.0	−1.5	−2.1	0.2	1.1
Excluding the former Soviet Union	0.9	0.4	1.6	2.4	2.3

a. Canada, France, Germany (West Germany through 1990, unified Germany thereafter), Italy, Japan, the United Kingdom, and the United States.
Source: World Bank global econometric modeling database.

Productivity growth in OECD countries has been slowing.

FIGURE 1.1   REAL GDP PER EMPLOYEE IN OECD COUNTRIES, 1964–92

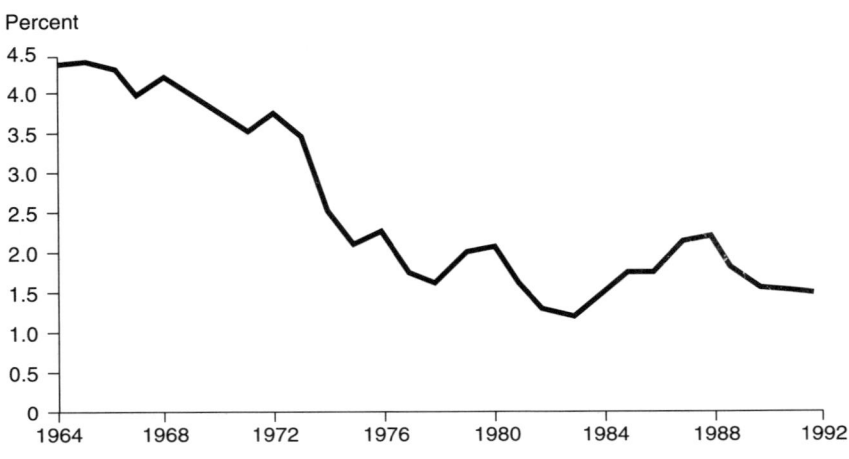

Source: World Bank staff estimates.

The association between the growth of per capita GDP in industrial coun-tries and that in the developing world has been close. In recent years, however, the developing countries in East Asia have managed to defy this association by relying on intraregional trade (table 1.2). During 1990–92, East Asia maintained its export and output growth despite the global recession (see tables A-1 through A-3 in the appendix), largely by expanding intraregional trade. But the substan-tial reduction in export growth in 1993 shows the limits to this effect and the continuing dependence on external factors. Industrial-country imports of man-ufactures from developing countries form a small share of their consumption—barely 3 percent—even though these imports are much larger in relation to value added in manufacturing. If developing countries follow outward-oriented policies and if industrial countries maintain open trading systems, developing-country exports of manufactures, including those from East Asia, can increase substantially during the rest of the 1990s and beyond.

East Asia is already big in sheer economic size, and it is rapidly growing bigger. Thus, the region is becoming a key player in the global economy. In purchasing power parity, it now accounts for about a quarter of global GDP. Its imports—worth close to $800 billion in 1992—are larger than those of the

In recent years, intraregional exports grew faster than the total.

TABLE 1.2   EAST ASIAN EXPORTS, 1990–92

Indicator	1990	1991	1992
Total exports (billions of dollars)	687	768	839
Export share (percent)			
Intraregional	38	40	41
Extraregional	62	60	59
Growth in exports (percent)			
Total	8.5	11.8	9.2
Intraregional	12.0	17.6	10.7

Source: World Bank staff estimates.

United States. Even more striking, East Asia is projected to account for two-fifths of incremental purchasing power and one-third to one-half of additional imports during 1992–2000 (table 1.3). Thus, what East Asia does really matters for global prospects.

Changes in the International Rules of the Game

The General Agreement on Tariffs and Trade has been the primary instrument in facilitating freer trade. Since the end of World War II, tariff rates around the world have fallen dramatically. Among the major industrial countries, weighted average tariffs have been lowered to less than 5 percent. But several areas of international trade remain in need of reform. The Uruguay Round of trade ne-

In the rest of the 1990s, East Asia is likely to account for at least a third of incremental imports.

TABLE 1.3   INCREASE IN IMPORTS, 1992–2000

Country group	Imports (billions of dollars) 1992	2000 (est.)	Increase	Percentage share of total increase
East Asia[a]	792	1,443	651	33
European Union	1,525	1,997	472	24
United States	553	922	369	19
Rest of the world	973	1,448	475	24

a. Based on conservative estimates.
Source: World Bank staff estimates.

gotiations addressed some of these issues, with fifteen working groups concerned with three broad areas:

- Increasing market access, including more open trade in agriculture and textiles (sectors that had received exceptional treatment within the GATT), and removing or reducing the remaining tariffs and quantitative restrictions, including voluntary export restraints and orderly marketing arrangements.
- Extending the GATT to new areas, principally trade in services and trade-related investment requirements imposed by governments, and enforcing intellectual property rights.
- Strengthening the GATT rules, especially those covering anti-dumping, subsidies, product standards, import licensing, safeguards (temporary import protection), and dispute settlement.

Reflecting these enlarged areas of activity, a new body, the World Trade Organization, is being created to guide reforms in international trade in goods, services, and intellectual property.

The recent success in the Uruguay Round offers important opportunities for developing-country exports, especially in such areas as agriculture. Progress in unraveling the multifiber arrangement (MFA) would also bring major benefits, especially for suppliers to world textile and apparel markets, although some countries might lose existing MFA rents. Tightened disciplines in gray areas of international trade and an improved safeguards code would also be important in limiting the proliferation of voluntary restraint arrangements.

With industrial-country tariff and quantitative restrictions to be reduced by 20 to 50 percent under the Uruguay Round, developing countries should experience aggregate export gains of about $50 billion (in 1988 prices)—mostly in labor-intensive manufactured articles, including clothing, footwear, and furniture. Of this $50 billion gain, East Asia might reap more than half, with 60 percent of that gain coming from textiles and clothing. The additional global gain in output by the turn of the century is expected to be some $250 billion a year, or 1 percent of the total output.

Even with the conclusion of the Uruguay Round, developing countries still face a tough trade environment, and implementing the Round will take time. The Round allows for very gradual incorporation of textiles and apparel into the GATT, over a transition period of ten years. Some 16 percent of 1990 imports are to be incorporated into the GATT at the outset of the program, increasing to 33 percent in 1996 and 51 percent in 2000. The remaining 49 percent of textile and clothing products are to see their quotas lifted only as of 2004. The agreement also allows for a small increase in the growth rate of quotas under the current MFA and for the obligation of all signatories to phase out non-MFA restrictions on textile imports. Special preferences have been set for the least developed countries, for small suppliers (with 1.2 percent or less of importing-country markets), and for natural-fiber producers.

Over the years, developing countries have claimed and received exemptions from GATT rules. By invoking Article XII to safeguard their balance of payments or Article XVIII to promote infant industries, developing countries can escape GATT disciplines—and get a free ride on global liberalization. Sustaining such special and differential treatment is becoming increasingly difficult. For example, it is not easy to maintain a code of rules if all participants do not adhere to it. In the long run, the rules for both industrial and developing countries will be the same—the major concession to developing countries grants them more time to bring their trading practices into line.

The subsidies code, for example, prohibits the use of subsidies to reward export performance. The least developed countries need not adhere to this prohibition, but other developing countries must comply within eight years. An explicit graduation rule in the subsidies code subjects developing countries with a per capita GDP of more than $1,000 to the same discipline as industrial countries. Other developing countries and the least developed countries will graduate sector by sector, as their world market share in a sector reaches 3.25 percent or more in consecutive years. They will, as noted, have eight years to adjust.

GATT agreements, especially for developing countries, may still contain many escape clauses, but the obligations of developing countries are also increasing. Regardless of the GATT rules in granting developing-country exclusions, industrial countries are not necessarily going to be lenient when enforcing their own antidumping and countervailing duty regulations.

So, whatever the benefits of the favored trade policies of the past, they are unlikely to be available in the future, particularly for East Asia. Given East Asia's dramatic growth in output and exports, Europe and the United States see the region as a competitor. With the globalization of technology and rapid movement of information, capital, and people, the industrial countries face tough competition from the developing countries, particularly from East Asia. The European Union (EU) and the United States have been experiencing rising unemployment (and in the United States, falling real wages). Their external deficits have also been rising (figure 1.2).

Even with most of the Western economies in recession, East Asian exports to them have been expanding at 15 to 20 percent a year. Imports from East Asian countries account for only part of the trade and output story of the developed countries, but it is often seen as a big part. East Asia's persistent trade surplus of well over $100 billion is thus politically unsustainable.

The recent unilateral policy stance of the United States is of particular concern to East Asia. Punitive actions initiated under Section 301 of the Trade

Domestic concerns in the United States and the European Union have strained their open trade policies.

FIGURE 1.2   CURRENT ACCOUNT BALANCE, UNEMPLOYMENT, AND WAGES IN THE UNITED STATES AND THE EUROPEAN UNION

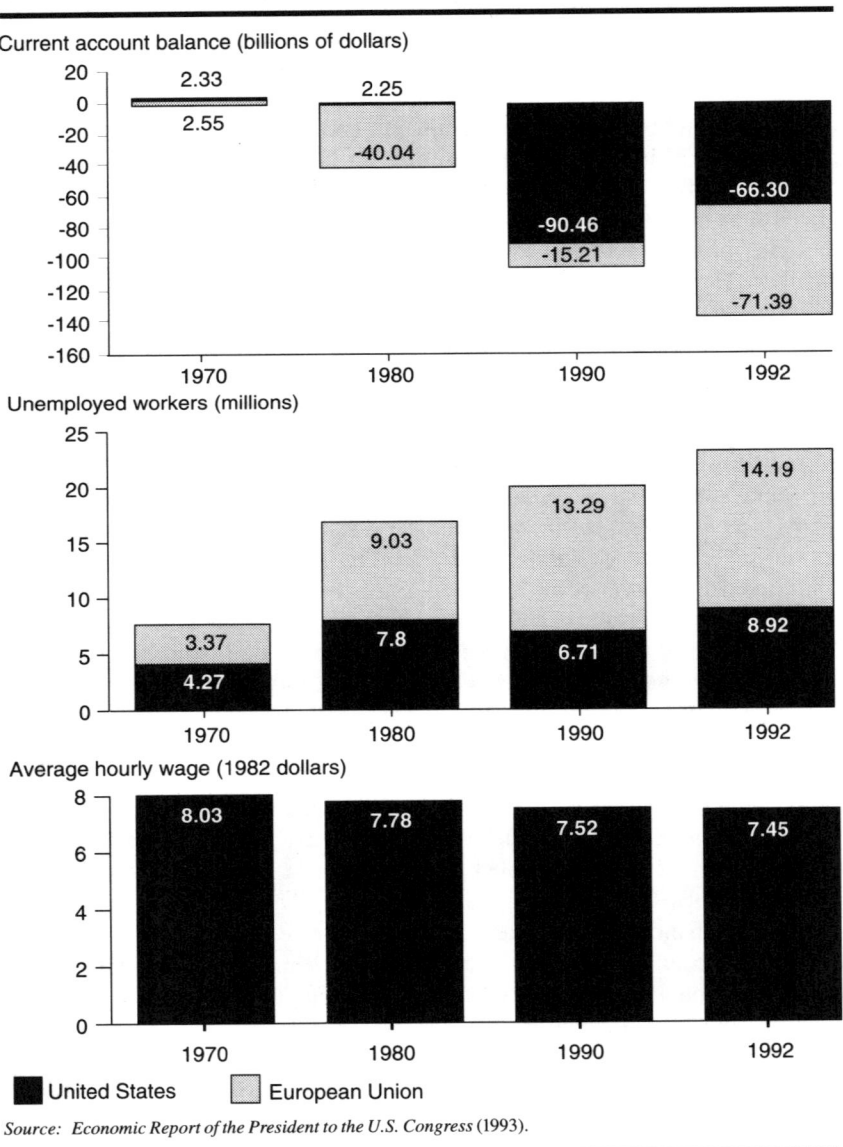

Source: Economic Report of the President to the U.S. Congress (1993).

Act in 1985 and more recently under the so-called Super 301 and Special 301 provisions have been contributing to trade tensions across the Pacific. Such unilateral actions result in a trading system that responds more to political pressures than to economic realities. An example of trade disputes is the case of steel (box 1.1).

The pressures for protectionism are prevalent in both industrial and developing countries. Trade liberalization is still viewed by some as a costly initiative, to be pursued only if others reciprocate. These potential and actual threats to openness suggest that it pays to underpin the progress in multilateralism with further reforms.

BOX 1.1   TRADE DISPUTES IN STEEL

The successful filing of seventy-two trade cases against twenty nations by U.S. steel producers in 1992—and the subsequent imposition of preliminary antidumping and countervailing duties on some of them—provoked the world steel community and triggered a counterresponse from Canada.

By June 1993, U.S. prices for steel had risen by an average of 20 percent. The benefits to carbon steel producers in the United States tempted special-steel producers to follow suit. Antidumping cases were filed against stainless steel wire-rod imports from Brazil, France, and India and against stainless pipe imports from Korea, Malaysia, and Taiwan (China). Further actions were threatened for stainless plate and bar imports.

Exporters retaliated. Brazil threatened to cut imports of U.S. metallurgical core if the U.S. International Trade Commission confirmed antidumping duties. In April 1993 Canada put provisional antidumping duties on imports of cold-rolled sheets from France, Germany, Italy, the United Kingdom, and the United States. These followed antidumping duties ranging from 4 to 130 percent imposed on hot-rolled sheets from six foreign producers, including the United States. Canada explicitly stated that none of these cases would have passed if U.S. mills had refrained from trade actions.

In the general atmosphere of protectionism, EU producers were also maintaining high barriers to Eastern Europe. At the end of April 1993, the EU Commission proposed a phased three-year quota regime for Czech and Slovak steel imports, plus punitive tariffs on any surplus above these quotas. Meanwhile, EU stockholders called for curbs on steel tube imports, while the EU set antidumping duties of up to 22 percent on seamless iron and steel tubes imported from Croatia, Hungary, and Poland. The situation was saved by the ruling of the U.S. Federal Trade Commission against most antidumping duties.

Experience suggests that the risks of protectionism and trade friction cannot be ignored. As chapter 5 shows, the potential losses from protectionism are large, especially for East Asia. The completion of the Uruguay Round is not cause for complacency. It is an opportunity to further strengthen the foundations of multilateralism. East Asia has much to gain from ensuring continued progress in multilateralism, and it is in a position to provide leadership in this direction.

CHAPTER TWO

East Asia's Economic Integration

EAST Asia's trading economy rests on three pillars. First, many East Asian economies depend on diverse human, natural, capital, and technological resources within and outside the region. They are too small or too narrowly endowed to be self-sufficient. Second, most East Asian countries, despite pursuing different development strategies, have encouraged international linkages. Third, with an outward orientation, East Asia has developed the infrastructure and business experience to coordinate international investment, production, and trade.

Origins of East Asian Integration

At the beginning of the twentieth century, regional interdependence in East Asia was substantial. In 1938, 67 percent of East Asia's trade was intraregional, compared with 41 percent today (Petri 1993). Most of this trade went through Hong Kong, Manila, Shanghai, and Singapore. These ports not only handled trade between the colonies and the European powers but also helped coordinate a vast network of commerce stretching from India to Japan. For example, Singapore mediated 70 percent of Thailand's trade, sending Thai rice to China and Japan in exchange for textiles from India and England.

East Asian interdependence continued to intensify between the two world wars, increasingly driven by Japanese economic and military power. Japan's linkages expanded rapidly with its Korean and Taiwanese territories. By 1932, Japan had displaced the Netherlands as Indonesia's largest trading partner and had made similar inroads in Malaysia at the expense of the United Kingdom. The stock of Japanese investments in China came to match that of Great Britain, as Japan began to develop Korea and Manchuria into complementary centers of industry. Manchuria, for example, produced coal, iron and steel, electricity and synthetic oil, rolling stock, and ships for itself and, in exchange for machinery, for Japan. Unlike Western colonial powers, Japan sought deep changes in the economic structure of its colonies and made large investments in transport and communications.

With war approaching in the late 1930s, East Asian interdependence took an ominous form. Plans were developed for an exclusive East Asian economic bloc and eventually for the notorious Greater East Asian Coprosperity Sphere. Not much came of these plans. Little economic integration was possible because war made sea transport unsafe. But the war highlighted the complementarity of the region's economies, weakening their ties to Western colonial powers and laying the foundation for postwar economic interdependence.

The war left East Asia in disarray. Disrupted by the collapse of prewar institutions and political relationships, insurrections, and civil war, trade flows abruptly shifted toward the United States. But the decline in trade among East Asian countries was due to the decline of East Asian economies—not to diminished preferences for intraregional trade.[3] Indeed, U.S. policy, recognizing that the collapse of the region's trade hindered economic recovery, attempted to revive trade within East and Southeast Asia with the help of U.S. aid and Japanese reparations.

Interdependence and Rapid Growth

Since the mid-1950s, East Asian trade patterns have become more focused on the Pacific area (figure 2.1). Trade within East Asia has followed a U-shaped pattern. Until the 1970s, the relative importance of trade within East Asia declined as the region developed stronger connections with North America and other countries. Eventually, however, the growth of the region's own markets began to outweigh the development of new markets, and internal East Asian trade began to increase again (see tables A-4 through A-6).

A somewhat different perspective on regional trade intensities in the Pacific comes from charting the evolution of gravity coefficients of regional linkages—coefficients that measure the extent of trade growth beyond that associated with the region's rapid output growth.[4] East Asia's economies were already highly interdependent in the early decades of this century, but that interdependence declined through most of the postwar period (figure 2.2). Interdependence in East Asia is still somewhat stronger than throughout the Pacific, but the two measures have converged.

The diversification of East Asia's trading relationships—the dominant trend of the postwar period—resulted from three reinforcing factors. The first

Since the mid-1950s, East Asia's trade within the Pacific region has increased as a share of its total trade.

FIGURE 2.1   EAST ASIAN TRADE, BY PARTNER, 1938–90

Percentage of total exports

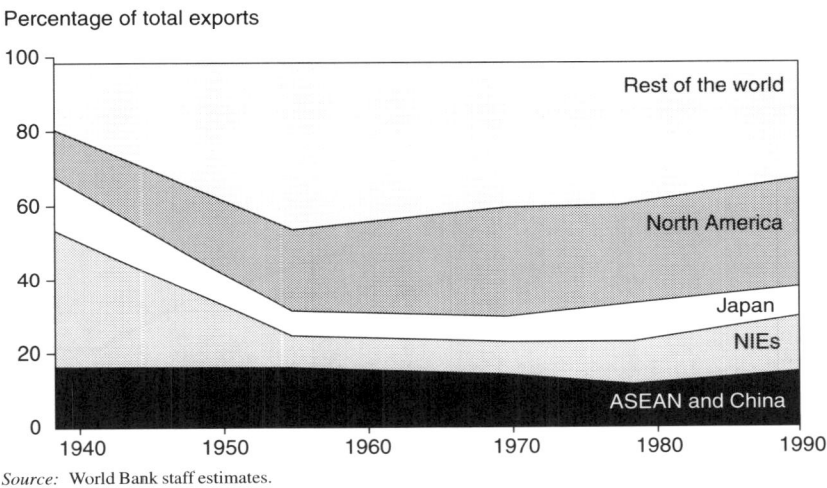

Source: World Bank staff estimates.

was the general integration of the global economy in the postwar period, spurred by several successful GATT rounds. The second was the region's rapid development. East Asian products gained greater acceptance abroad, and the region's contacts with foreign markets were facilitated by improved transport, communications, and marketing experience. The third was the similarity of East Asian development patterns. With the region's developing economies becoming competitive in similar products, they could not look to each other for markets. These factors helped expand East Asia's trade network and contributed to particularly strong links across the Pacific.

The intensity of East Asian trade links, after a long decline, is on the rise. Estimates of the size of the turnaround depend on the measures used and the time periods studied (see box 2.1). But since the 1960s, intraregional trade has accounted for an increasingly large share of all trade by East Asian countries and of total world trade. Why the turnaround? East Asia is trading more internally simply because its markets have become so important. Rising costs in Japan and the newly industrializing economies have shifted industries to other East Asian countries, increasing the trade in components and machinery. More liberal trade and investment policies are opening East Asian markets, though

The intensity, or bias, of East Asia's intraregional trade has declined.

FIGURE 2.2   INTENSITY OF REGIONAL TRADE, EAST ASIA
AND THE PACIFIC REGION, 1938–90

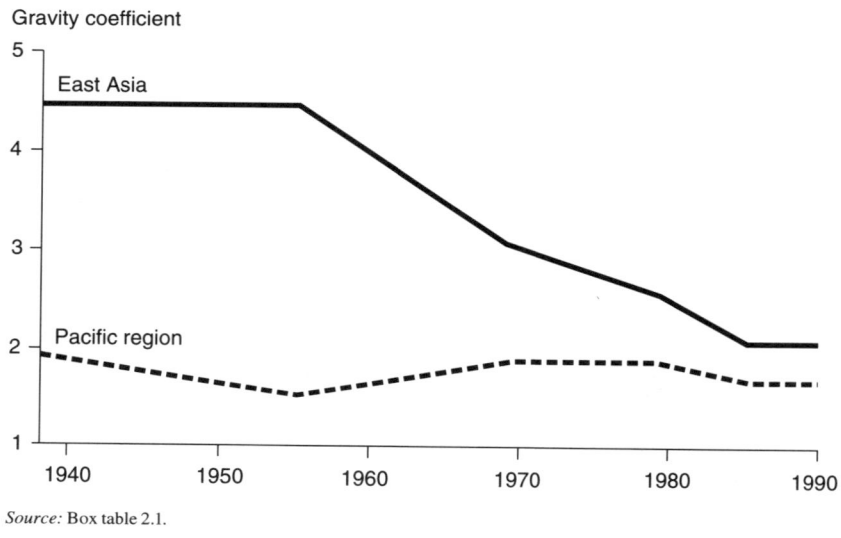

Gravity coefficient

Source: Box table 2.1.

scope remains for more action. And changes in the strategies of large and small firms seem to increase the scope for intraregional trade.

Today's Pacific trade network encompasses a wide range of close economic relationships—some based on proximity and history, others on comparative advantage, especially in labor costs, and still others on intraindustry trade between similar economies. The links based on geographical or historical ties, measured by gravity coefficients, have been weakening in East Asia (box table 2.1), except for the China–Hong Kong relationship. Links based on comparative advantage and specialization have been growing stronger, mainly among the NIEs. The strongest among them are:

- Japanese export links to Korea, Malaysia, Taiwan (China), and Thailand.
- Japanese import links to Korea, Taiwan (China), and ASEAN.
- Korean and Taiwanese export links to the United States and other industrial countries.

BOX 2.1   IS EAST ASIA BECOMING MORE
INTERDEPENDENT?

Considerable interest has recently been focused on whether East Asia is changing its economic orientation toward intraregional linkages. The popular perception of a major shift of this sort is not fully supported by empirical evidence. While the share of intra-regional trade is increasing, this is due mostly to the rapid economic growth of the region and not to greater preferences for the region's own products.

Part of the difficulty is that different analysts use different measures of interdependence. Some view growth in the region's internal trade as evidence of stronger linkages. Others point to recent increases in the *share* of intra-

BOX TABLE 2.1   MEASURES OF REGIONAL INTERDEPENDENCE
THROUGH TWO-WAY TRADE

Region	1938	1955	1969	1979	1985	1990
Absolute measure: intraregional trade as a percentage of total world trade						
East Asia	10.0	2.2	2.9	4.2	6.4	7.9
North America	3.0	6.7	6.9	4.2	6.4	5.3
Pacific region	18.0	13.5	16.9	15.6	24.8	24.6
Western Europe	18.2	19.6	28.7	29.3	27.1	33.8
Relative measure: intraregional trade as a percentage of regional trade						
East Asia	67.1	31.3	29.3	33.2	36.3	40.7
North America	22.7	33.4	37.9	28.7	33.0	31.3
Pacific region	58.3	45.0	56.6	54.5	64.3	64.9
Western Europe	46.1	49.1	64.7	66.4	65.4	71.2
Double-relative measure: gravity coefficient						
East Asia	4.5	4.5	3.0	2.6	2.1	2.1
North America	1.7	1.7	2.1	2.0	1.7	1.8
Pacific region	1.9	1.5	1.9	1.9	1.7	1.7
Western Europe	1.2	1.2	1.5	1.5	1.6	1.5

Source: Petri (1993).

(Box continues on the following page.)

These production links have generally intensified and begun to spread rapidly to China and Southeast Asia, the next tier of the region's manufacturing economies.

Links among economies at similar levels of development, strong within North America and Oceania, are moderately important between North America and Japan but weaker than among similarly closely associated industrial countries in Europe. Links among other Pacific region countries with similar incomes tend to be weak. For example, no large gravity coefficients are found among the four NIEs; the gravity coefficients are mostly below the region's

Box 2.1 (continued)

regional trade in the region's overall trade. Still others look to evidence that the region prefers its products to those made elsewhere.

However, certain trends can be identified in the different measures (box table 2.1):

■ The *absolute measure*, which compares East Asia's internal trade to world trade, increased nearly fourfold between 1955 and 1990, though it is still not as high as it was just before World War II.

■ The *relative measure*, which compares the region's internal trade to its total trade, has traced a U-shaped course, falling from a pre-war high of 67 percent to a low of 29 percent in the 1960s, rising to more than 40 percent today.

■ The *double-relative measure* (also called a gravity or intensity coefficient), compares the share of the region in its own market to its share in worldwide trade. This measure, which estimates the region's bias toward its own products, shows no clear recent trend. Frankel (1992) found no increase in the intensity of the region's intraregional trade bias between 1980

and 1989. But Petri (1993) showed that the stability of the intensity index in the 1980s is itself noteworthy, since the index has been falling steadily and sharply since World War II. Indeed, Petri's data show a breaking point in 1985 and a slight increase since then. A recent study by the United States International Trade Commission (USITC 1993) finds some variability but no strong trend in recent data. Whatever the outcome of this debate, it is clear that East Asia is well integrated compared with both North America and Western Europe and that it has not yet witnessed the kind of trade intensification that occurred in Europe after the European Union was established.

Which of these measures is most useful? It depends on the question. From the viewpoint of trade policy, what may matter most is the rapid rise in the relative measure—the trade share of interdependence. As more of the region's trade is destined for its own markets, the region's companies and governments are more likely to undertake investments in contacts, infrastructure, and policies that support intraregional trade. Such investments themselves contribute to the further intensification of intraregional relationships.

---

overall index of 2.1, except exports from Taiwan (China) to Hong Kong, probably destined for China. Nor are there large gravity coefficients among the region's lower-income countries (most of the gravity coefficients in the bloc formed by China, Indonesia, the Philippines, and Thailand are below 1). Except for some modest increase in intra-ASEAN trade, these horizontal links have generally weakened.

Together, these regional links have contributed much to East Asian growth. They have enabled many countries to pursue highly successful outward-oriented development strategies. And they have enabled countries to upgrade their industrial structures by shifting to more advanced manufactured products. Both the flexibility of markets and regional flows of technology and capital were important in this process.

East Asia's outward orientation was accomplished in various ways, ranging from the virtual elimination of trade barriers in Hong Kong and Singapore to the aggressive policies of export promotion in Korea and Taiwan (China). Along the way, all of the region's successful developing countries became highly trade-oriented by international standards. East Asian economies became considerably more dependent on trade after 1970, with trade gains substantially larger than for the world as a whole (figure 2.3).

The region's outward-oriented policies would have been much tougher to implement without the Pacific's enabling international environment. This envi-

East Asia's export orientation has been increasing since 1970.

FIGURE 2.3   OUTWARD ORIENTATION OF SELECTED COUNTRY GROUPS

Ratio of trade to GDP (percent)

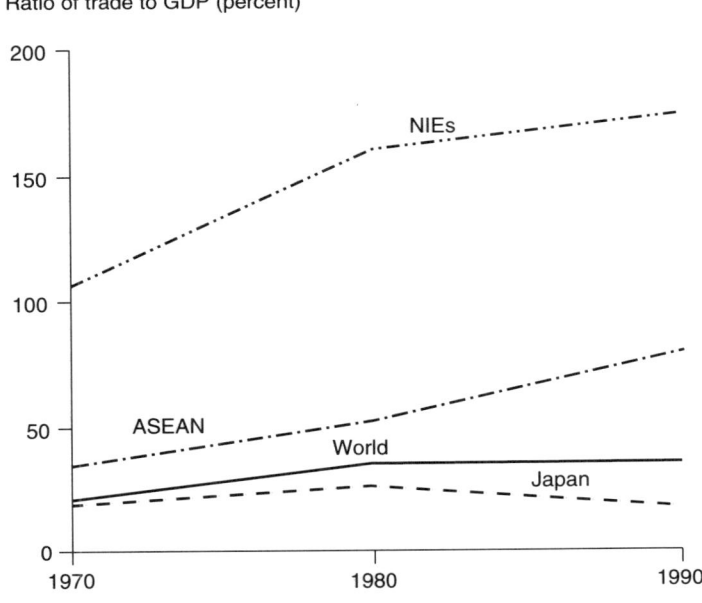

Source: World Bank staff estimates.

ronment supplied capital and technology and offered large, accommodating markets. Foreign investments from Japan, the United States, and eventually the NIEs provided the experience and know-how needed to connect several East Asian economies to world markets. The large, open markets of North America helped to absorb new production.

East Asia's outward-oriented growth has been remarkable. Over the past quarter century, its exports rose from less than $30 billion to about $850 billion. (See table A-7 for a breakdown of exports by commodity, and table A-8 for a breakdown of imports.) Somewhat less than half the increase in exports can be attributed to the region's growth in economic activity, and somewhat more than half to its increased outward orientation. Approximately 45 percent of East Asia's exports can be attributed to the region's penetration of non–East Asian markets, especially North America. From 1965 to 1990, East Asia's two-way trade with North America rose from about 11 percent of GDP to 21 percent, and the share of North America's imports from East Asia climbed from 17 percent of the total to 33 percent. Toward the end of the 1980s, the United States was running a large global trade deficit, including deficits with every Pacific country except Australia. East Asia's export growth thus hinged on the large, accommodating shift in U.S. production and trade.

East Asian exports shifted first from primary to manufactured products and then from light to more advanced manufactures. The more advanced countries made way for these gains by losing market shares—in the United States in virtually all manufactured products and in Japan and the NIEs in lower-end manufactures—a good illustration of Akamatsu's (1960) "flying geese" hypothesis. In this model, countries develop increasingly sophisticated industries by accumulating capital and technology. In the process, they capture exports previously produced by more advanced economies, as those economies also move up the ladder. In part, these developments reflect economic adaptations to changing factor endowments, and countries are helped by following—that is, by copying the successful policies and technologies of neighboring countries (Petri 1992a). Close ties through trade, culture, and history have helped East Asian countries take advantage of each other's experience in production, marketing, management, and policymaking.

East Asian countries may have followed similar development trajectories because of externalities in export market development. Pacific countries seem well placed to take over markets previously held by other countries in the region. U.S. markets for television sets have been passed down from Japan to the NIEs—and from the NIEs to China and the Southeast Asian countries. This process is sometimes set in motion by explicit quotas—typically, voluntary export restraints—on the exports of a country that initially developed a market. And often, this is facilitated by foreign direct investment by the pioneering exporter, when protection or cost increases make it impossible to continue competing from its home base.

This sequential industrialization pattern evolved remarkably smoothly over the past twenty-five years. Japan, the NIEs, China, and the more advanced Southeast Asian manufacturers followed each other in a range of industries and markets without any sign of losing their momentum. By moving to higher rungs, each economy left lower rungs of the ladder to less advanced economies. And countries all along the ladder have been able to upgrade their manufacturing relatively free of market constraints—as fast as their investments in technology and capital would permit.

Trade has played a vital role in the structural development of East Asian economies. Today the region's prospects are crucially linked to openness in trade and investment. It is in the region's interest to take initiatives that strengthen linkages both within the region and with the trading partners outside.

CHAPTER THREE

Trade Reform in East Asia

$\mathbf{I}$N earlier phases of their development, several successful East Asian economies combined export development with import protection. Japan, Korea, and Taiwan (China), for instance, provided substantial import protection to their infant industries through trade barriers and financial incentives. Development theories in the 1950s and 1960s endorsed this approach, which also had the implicit or explicit support of multilateral organizations, including the GATT.

Although most East Asian economies gradually opened up their markets, the trend toward liberalization has not been consistent across countries or over time. For example, protection in several East Asian countries actually increased in the 1970s (Bhattacharya and Linn 1988). The effective rate of protection is estimated to have more than doubled in some cases between 1971 and 1980, with consumer goods and transport equipment accounting for much of the increase. In Korea, effective protection was higher in 1978 than in 1968. There was also considerable dispersion in those rates, with the highest levels applying to transport, consumer durables, machinery, and heavy intermediate goods. The Philippines had high and variable protection. In Indonesia, policies during the 1970s provided more protection for the large investments financed by the oil boom. In Malaysia, protection remained moderate, although there were exceptions for transport equipment, machinery, fabricated products, and industrial chemicals. Hong Kong and Singapore had low protection.[5]

On the whole, successful East Asian economies gradually liberalized trade. The process of liberalization continues. The impact on economic growth is perhaps more discernible in East Asia than elsewhere in the world, presumably because of more comprehensive and sustained actions. Also notable in the region's outstanding economic performance is the strong role of the state in supporting export development. Looking ahead, both liberalization and government efforts to ensure adequate regulatory frameworks will be important.

Trade Reforms in the 1980s

The economic costs of protection, though well known, were dramatized as the protected economies got into fiscal and balance-of-payments difficulties in the 1980s. Although East Asia did far better in avoiding crises than did other regions, it too felt the inefficiency of protection. And with the maturing of the region's industries, it too was politically ready to liberalize trade in the 1980s.

The consensus among development theorists was moving toward trade liberalization. Multilateral institutions, particularly the International Monetary Fund and the World Bank, supported liberalization through both funding and policy advice. Usually, a country regards the easing of import restrictions as a cost, to be undertaken only if compensating benefits will be provided by its trading partners in the form of their trade liberalization. But in the context of adjustment programs, unilateral trade liberalization was accepted as good for the country, with adjustment funding helping to meet the transitional costs.

The results of this approach have been impressive. With some trade liberalization, Indonesia and Thailand have witnessed a rapid shift to manufactured exports. China has had tremendous success in building trade, especially through the special economic zones, which are allowed much freer trade than in the rest of the economy. Trade has also grown remarkably rapidly in the already open economies of Hong Kong, Malaysia, Singapore, and Taiwan (China).

Korea reduced its (unweighted) average tariffs from about 32 percent in 1982 to 22 percent in 1985 and to about 10 percent in 1992, and the coverage of quantitative restrictions was reduced to less than 5 percent. Agricultural protection, however, remained much higher than these averages suggest. Trade reforms are continuing, with further reductions in tariffs and quantitative restrictions planned through 1997.

Korea's trade reforms worked well for several reasons. First, the earlier export development provided an important cushion for the balance of payments. Second, because of the emphasis on export competitiveness, domestic firms were in many instances already competitive at the time of liberalization. Third, the government adhered to the announced liberalization schedule—and even when exports weakened and the balance of payments widened, as in 1985, it used offsetting tariff increases only sparsely. Fourth, macroeconomic stability and a realistic real exchange rate underpinned the liberalization of imports.

In the Philippines the average nominal tariff was reduced from more than 40 percent in 1980 to about 24 percent in 1992, and the dispersion narrowed from 0 to 100 percent in 1980 to 10 to 50 percent, with a few exceptions. Many consumer goods were removed from the banned import list. Trade reform, aborted during the severe balance-of-payments difficulties in 1983, resumed in 1986 following a major stabilization. Of the 1,232 import items that were originally to have been liberalized in the early 1980s, 936 were liberalized during 1986. Indirect tax reforms since then have eliminated most of the aspects of the domestic tax structure that discriminated against imports. Further reforms are anticipated, especially in removing quantitative restrictions in several categories, including agriculture.

Indonesia had an average tariff of about 35 percent in 1984, with a range between 0 and 225 percent, coupled with quantitative restrictions covering a fifth of all imports. In 1985 the tariff ceiling was reduced from 225 to 60 percent, with tariffs for most products ranging from 5 to 35 percent. And the coverage of import items under licensing or quantitative restrictions was reduced. The import reforms announced later represented a fundamental shift toward tariffs. Recently, the average tariff has been about 20 percent, and quantitative restrictions have covered about 10 percent of import items (but a quarter of domestic value added). Further progress is envisaged in eliminating quantitative restrictions and in lowering the still-high protection for manufacturing.

Thailand's tariff reform program of 1982 was slowed initially because of a general import surcharge and in April 1985 because of offsetting tariff adjustments. As a result, the average nominal protection was higher in the late 1980s than before 1982. Thailand is now rationalizing its tariff and tax regime.

The Scope for Further Reform

With parity and reciprocity becoming the watchwords of trade discussions among East Asian countries (and throughout the world), the region would do well to further reduce protective measures. East Asia's trade regimes still have more elements of protection than do those of its industrial trading partners. Several developing East Asian countries still have substantial tariff rates, even after taking into account the agreements of the Uruguay Round. Even more significant, the effective rates of protection, particularly in manufacturing, have been relatively high in some East Asian countries (table 3.1).

In several East Asian economies, visible trade barriers are low or declining. The key issues are restrictions and internal policies regarding trade flows. The effect of these measures on openness to foreign trade has been a subject of much controversy, and any conclusions are beyond the scope of this report. It can be said, however, that there is a trade-off between exchange rate adjustments and quantitative restrictions. If the large trade surpluses of some of the East Asian economies persist, there will be pressure for their currencies to appreciate, hurting exports and income growth.

Nominal protection is moderately high—and effective protection higher.

TABLE 3.1   TRADE PROTECTION IN FIVE EAST ASIAN COUNTRIES

Country	Unweighted average nominal tariff (percent)	Import items subject to import restrictions	Effective protection rate in manufacturing (percent)
Indonesia (1992)	20	<5	52
Korea (1992)	10	<5	28[a]
Malaysia (1990)	<10	<5	23[a]
Philippines (1992)	24	3	32
Thailand (1992)	28[b]	<5	51[c]

a. This estimate is for 1988.
b. Trade-weighted. An earlier, unweighted estimate for 1989 was 39 percent.
c. This estimate is for 1988; it excludes agroprocessing and is weighted by value added in world prices. Using the more standard weighting of value added at domestic prices yields a rate of 61 in 1988. Reforms since then are considered to have lowered this estimate significantly.
Source: World Bank country reports; GATT; Government of Australia.

OECD.   The OECD countries outside East Asia have made substantial progress in lowering tariffs and most quantitative restrictions. But restrictions have remained, such as the large agricultural protection in the European Union and certain manufacturing quotas there and in the United States. And in some respects trade restrictiveness increased in the 1980s in the OECD countries, with discriminatory practices such as antidumping measures, safeguards, and countervailing duties becoming more common. The completion of the Uruguay Round signals progress in these areas. North America and the European Union can do a great deal to further openness by refraining from actual or potential unilateral actions, discriminatory regionalism, and protectionism.

Japan.   Despite recent progress, reform in the trade area continues to be important in Japan. Tariffs have peaked at up to 60 percent for some treated leather and leather footwear and are as high as 20 percent for wood products, textiles and clothing items, some aluminum products, and paper; tariff rates on agricultural products average 12 percent. Import quotas have remained on state-controlled trading in agricultural products such as rice, wheat, and dairy products. Moreover, as formal barriers to trade have fallen in manufacturing, international concern has shifted to the impact of informal barriers. Trading partners continue to focus on Japan's government procurement practices, quality standards and testing requirements, customs procedures, administrative guidance, antimonopoly legislation, and the distribution system.

China.   At the top of the list of East Asian countries able to launch bold trade liberalization programs in the 1990's is China. The special economic zones have introduced liberalization to limited parts of the economy, with dramatic effect. Now the economy is poised to go further.

- De jure trade restrictions in China are high—in both tariffs and quantitative restrictions (World Bank 1994a).
- There is much redundancy in these import barriers, and Chinese industries in a broad range of import categories are globally competitive.
- A bold program of import liberalization can improve the efficiency of state-owned enterprises and contribute to China's drive to become a full member of the international trading community.
- In January 1992 the government announced sizable reductions in tariff levels on 225 tariff lines and the abolition of the import regulatory duty. Even with these reductions, tariff rates in China remained relatively high, with an average unweighted tariff rate of 43 percent and a weighted rate of 32 percent (table 3.2). Further progress was made in lowering tariffs and other import restrictions in 1993 and early 1994.

Quantitative restrictions comprise import licenses, import controls, and import monopolies through designated national trading companies—many of which overlap, making the exact application difficult to disentangle. Responsi-

In China, statutory tariff rates have remained high for many commodities.

TABLE 3.2   AVERAGE TARIFF FOR SELECTED GOODS, CHINA, 1992
(percent)

Commodity	Unweighted average tariff	Trade-weighted average tariff
Art and antiques	30	2
Footwear	86	78
Hides and leather	58	29
Miscellaneous manufactures	67	74
Textiles and textile products	73	61
Transport and motor vehicles	43	57
Overall average	**43**	**32**

Source: World Bank (1994a).

bility for implementing these measures is widely dispersed within central and local governments; for example, ore imports, in some cases, require approvals from many different agencies.

Despite China's protective trade policies, tariff collection rates are low. In 1991 China collected duties of only 5.6 percent of the cost, insurance, and freight value of imports—lower than the rate in most developing countries—in large part because of import duty exemptions and rebates. However, in most countries, low collection rates imply high effective rates of protection because exemptions are generally for inputs and not for competing imports.

China has made much progress and should be able to make further deep cuts in tariffs and quantitative restrictions without major contractions even in the most protected sectors, such as textiles and machinery. Doing so should reduce production costs and improve China's export performance. Moreover, given China's good prospects for exports and the availability of external capital flows, including FDI, the headroom in the balance of payments for increasing imports is quite large. Greater openness should help China reduce the current inflationary pressures and increase the market discipline of state-owned enterprises.

Indonesia.   Despite considerable progress since the mid-1980s, the Indonesian trade system has remained quite protective for some subsectors. The numerous tariff categories have given the impression of a made-to-measure code. An example is the high tariff applied to motor vehicles and motorcycles, which also received protection from import surcharges and quantitative restrictions. The median tariff has been 20 percent, but the dispersion remains high, with a standard deviation of 17 percentage points from the average tariff. The coverage of quantitative restrictions has been reduced since 1986.

Some industries have reduced effective protection since 1987 (table 3.3). Tariff reductions and the deregulation of cotton imports have improved the competitive position of the textile sector, but protection remained high in food and beverage sectors. Reducing the barriers to trade and investment in agriculture would allow the food industry to prosper and would lower food prices for Indonesian consumers. Consumer prices for wheat flour are significantly higher than import parity prices, and the prices that factories pay are artificially lower. The retail price of sugar has been 30 to 100 percent higher than world prices over the past 20 years. And for soybeans, Indonesians paid 38 percent more than the import parity price in 1990.

The benefits of import liberalization—lower prices, lower production costs, and increased competitiveness of nontraditional exports—are well documented. And Indonesia continues to carry out trade and domestic liberalization, with a view to strengthening export and overall economic performance. As in

In Indonesia, effective protection rates in manufacturing have been high.

TABLE 3.3   EFFECTIVE PROTECTION RATES IN MANUFACTURING, INDONESIA
(percent)

Type of manufacturing	1987	1990	1992
Engineering	152	139	82
Food, beverages, and tobacco	122	126	120
Nonmetal products	57	49	44
Textiles	102	35	34
Wood products	25	33	33
Other manufacturing	124	79	80
Overall average	**68**	**59**	**52**

Source: World Bank country studies.

other countries, some of the constraints to further action have been political in nature. On the economic side, revenue and balance-of-payments considerations can be addressed by implementing revenue-enhancing measures and by developing export-oriented FDI.

Korea.   Following steady liberalization over a decade, the average tariff was about 10 percent in 1992. But many products have been subject to a tariff rate of 30 percent or higher—for example, meat, poultry, most fruits and nuts, many fresh and processed vegetables, and various vegetable oils. High tariffs have also affected some industrial products, such as soda ash, and import licensing (through quotas or bans) applies to about 15 percent of imported goods, primarily agricultural and fish products but also paper. Many high-value or processed agricultural products have also been affected by secondary barriers, such as food safety regulations and excessively slow and arbitrary customs and quarantine clearance procedures. Nonetheless, Korea has been continuing the process of opening up.

Malaysia.   Overall, the country has achieved a considerable degree of openness, with low import duties on most manufactured goods. But tariffs on most high-value agricultural products have remained relatively steep—at 20 percent—and duties have been especially high on some food and agricultural items. Malaysia has also maintained a short list of prohibited manufactured imports to protect its "pioneer industries," including automobiles.

The Philippines.   Quantitative restrictions on imports—mostly requirements for prior approval by various government agencies—affected almost

3,000 items in 1980 (36 percent of customs categories); in 1992, 150 items (about 2.5 percent of customs categories) were covered. Regulated items fell from 33 percent of total imports in 1981 to 13 percent in 1990. The restricted items of greatest economic interest are agricultural goods and goods related to rationalization programs for industry, cars, jeeps, and motorcycles. In 1992 the unweighted average tariff rate was less than 25 percent (see table 3.1) There nevertheless is scope for further reform of tariffs and quantitative restrictions and the development of exports as part of the continuing program for reform.

Taiwan (China). Progress in reducing the tariff on nonagricultural products has been considerable, and the average nominal tariff rate is about 9 percent. But average tariffs on agricultural products have been 22 percent, and fresh fruit and processed agricultural products often faced substantial import duties. Some industrial products are also subject to high tariffs. The average duty has been 20 percent for automotive parts, and the effective duty and tax rate for passenger cars and trucks ranges from 60 to 100 percent. Taiwan (China) has also continued to maintain an import licensing system. Two-thirds of the items in the tariff schedule could be imported without a license in recent years. Of the remaining one-third, a majority required only pro forma import visas from commercial banks, while a small number of items required import licenses from the Board of Foreign Trade.

Thailand. Economic growth over the past twenty years has been impressive, as Thailand's trade policies have gradually become less protectionist. The wide dispersion of its tariff rates has resulted in high effective protection for some manufacturing subsectors—agroprocessing, food products, leather products, chemicals, textiles, and motor vehicles—and the implementation of tariff policy often has been discretionary. Thailand has done remarkably well in attracting FDI and increasing exports. A more transparent and coherent trade regime would seem to be needed to improve efficiency and sustain growth and to preempt unilateral and bilateral pressures from the country's major trading partners. And Thailand has been pursuing a policy of liberalization in order to maintain the country's export and overall economic performance.

Revenues from import duties have accounted for about one-quarter of tax revenue. The budget surplus since 1988 has given the government greater flexibility in resuming import liberalization through substantial tariff reform. Thailand has also made progress in reducing import bans (for example, on unfinished garments and certain vinyl chloride mixtures) and in replacing quantitative measures by tariff-based measures (for example, on soybean cakes and fish meal). About 100 product categories—corresponding to about 8 percent of all four-digit harmonized system categories—have been affected by import licensing. In recent years, roughly a quarter of these were agricultural commodities, including such important exports as rice and sugar. Of the industrial products, import licensing covered items such as some textiles, some machinery, motor vehicles, paper products, and chemicals.

Viet Nam. A World Bank study (1993b) suggests that (a) the current trade regime has substantial tariff and quantitative restrictions; (b) import liberalization will be easier now than later because the vested interests in local industries have not yet become entrenched; and (c) the prospects for exports and external capital flows, including FDI, are bright enough to accommodate the initial increase in imports following trade liberalization.

Viet Nam's tariff structure, though amended in 1992 and again in 1993, is cascaded like that of most developing countries in the 1960s and 1970s. While machinery, equipment, and medicine have had negligible tariffs, garments, footwear, soft drinks, cigarettes, cosmetics, and cars have had tariffs as high as 50–150 percent. For manufactured goods, the tariff rates seem to increase with the degree of fabrication.

Viet Nam also has considerable quantitative restrictions—foreign trade permits for imports and exports, a license for each shipment, and quotas for some commodities. The number of trading permits increased from about 30 in 1988 to 800 in 1992 for state-owned enterprises, but none were issued to private firms, despite private exports accounting for a growing share of trade. Private firms have had to export through an authorized trading company with direct trading rights. Import quotas are applied mainly to cars, motorbikes, and assembly kits for motorbikes, electronics, and refrigeration equipment.

Viet Nam obtains only about 8 percent of its revenues from import tariffs, so the loss of revenue is not a constraint on trade liberalization. Nor are major enterprises that supply such goods as electronics, refrigeration equipment, and automobiles likely to be particularly affected. Import liberalization will thus not risk disrupting domestic production of such items. On the contrary, Viet Nam's recent export growth provides a strong basis for export-led growth, assisted by liberal trade and foreign investment regimes. The current reform agenda is pursuing this goal.

Commodity Patterns of Protection

Protection of domestic industries can arise for different reasons, depending on the type of commodity. For agriculture, some protection is inspired by social, political, and security interests. For simple manufactures, protection is a hangover from the earlier period of infant-industry development. For sophisticated manufactures, protection is for infant industries. For luxury goods, the main objective is to reduce consumption and to tax the wealthy.

Protection of agriculture.   Many developing countries actually tax, rather than protect, agricultural producers, while they protect manufacturing industries. China, Indonesia, the Philippines, and Thailand follow this pattern, with protection in manufacturing higher than that in agriculture. In these cases, leveling the playing field for farmers is the priority. Japan, Korea, and Taiwan (China), by contrast, have protected agriculture against foreign imports and provided it with various kinds of subsidies.

In most East Asian countries, labor productivity and manufacturing wages have been rising rapidly. Growth in agriculture has been more uneven. Some countries have been especially concerned with the problem of protecting relative incomes in agricultural and rural sectors and reducing the pressure for urban migration, as well as with national security concerns about depending on foreign countries for basic foodstuffs. In these countries the reduction of protection for agriculture has been slow. The process can be expedited if agricultural investments can speed productivity improvements so the pace of liberalization is connected with the availability of funds for investment in agriculture. In addition, the case for liberalization will be strengthened when the industrial countries reduce subsidization of their agriculture and allow market determination of prices for agricultural products.

In general, the East Asian countries have remarkable complementarity for meeting their needs for agricultural goods. The thickly populated economies of China, Hong Kong, Japan, Korea, Singapore, Taiwan (China), and Viet Nam can do well by specializing in manufactures and relying on imports of agricultural goods from countries with better land endowments—Australia, Canada, Indonesia, New Zealand, the Philippines, Thailand, and the United States.

Protection of simple manufactures.   Many East Asian countries that emerged as major exporters of simple manufactures, such as textiles and footwear, also protect these industries heavily. To some extent, this may be the result of inertia in adapting trade policies to changing circumstances. The simple manufactures, the infants of earlier years, were granted protection in line with the approach prevailing at that time. For most East Asian countries, liberalizing trade in these sectors should be a high priority. To the extent that East Asian economies have become competitive in these manufactures, the pressure of external competition should not be disruptive.

Protection of sophisticated manufactures.   Most East Asian countries continue to heavily protect sophisticated manufactures, such as electronics, machinery, and transport equipment. The main justification is the need to protect infant industries—and the benefits of learning-by-doing behind trade barriers. The experience of China, Japan, and Korea supports this approach, and developing countries are unlikely to give up the protection without a credible alternative for acquiring technology. That alternative exists: industry can now be promoted more effectively through FDI than through import substitution. China is using FDI for development of competitive industries in textiles and electronics. FDI promotion will be helped by liberal trade regimes, and FDI will in turn create economic and political pressures for liberal trade regimes. This virtuous circle could be the key to the future development of sophisticated manufacturers in East Asia.

Protection of luxury and discouraged goods.   In several East Asian countries, high tariffs and other barriers are imposed on imports of such goods as tobacco, alcohol, and cosmetics. If equally high taxes are not imposed on domestic production, the system is likely to end up increasing the domestic production of these discouraged goods. Once production is in place, discouraging consumption is much more difficult, both economically and politically. So, the case is strong for taxation parity between imports and the domestic production of these commodities.

■ ■ ■

Most East Asian countries have come of age in trade. In many industries, they are internationally competitive, and in many others, increased openness is augmenting productivity. The infant-industry arguments are less and less plausible for most of developing East Asia, particularly because of the new dynamics of technology transfers and foreign investment flows, the subject matter of the next chapter.

Reform of Investment Regimes

THE prices of capital and labor in Hong Kong, Korea, Singapore, and Taiwan (China) are rapidly moving toward OECD levels. There have been significant labor movements—legal and illegal—across national borders in recent years, and these are likely to accelerate as labor shortages emerge, especially in the industrial countries (box 4.1). The movement of capital is also gathering momentum in East Asia, transforming the region's economic landscape. A virtuous circle now links foreign direct investment and the expansion of trade. The features of this link are best seen from the country experiences.

Japan, Korea, and Taiwan (China) permitted only modest amounts of inward direct investment in their early development. The emphasis was on developing indigenous technological capability and nurturing domestic markets. There were also concerns about the political and social implications of large inflows of FDI. But few East Asian nations still view FDI as a threat to national sovereignty. On the contrary, they see it as an effective conduit for technology transfers and as a means to secure access to overseas markets. Cultural affinities between suppliers and recipients of FDI also smooth the path for intraregional investment.

Trends and Determinants of FDI

FDI inflows (net of repatriation) to developing East Asia increased from about $3 billion in 1986 to $19 billion in 1992—from 33 percent of total external resource inflows to 38 percent. Developing East Asia's share of total FDI to developing countries increased from about 24 percent in 1986 to about 38 per-

BOX 4.1   LABOR MIGRATION IN EAST ASIA

With rapid growth of output in East Asia, labor shortages are emerging, and labor migration is playing a part in regional integration. The region has been one of the largest suppliers of emigrant labor to the world. But its own record in freeing labor flows into the region has been poor, with many restrictions regulating immigrants and foreign residency. As East Asia moves toward European levels of integration in trade, these policies will have to be reviewed and adjusted.

Official statistics considerably understate the size of the immigrant labor force. Japan's Ministry of Justice estimated in 1992 that some 310,000 legal and illegal workers were in the country. About 90,000 were legal workers on permits, and some 70,000 were students and trainees, many of whom were employed part-time. This points to about 150,000 illegal workers, according to official estimates, but private estimates put the number as high as 300,000, more than the number of officially recorded migrant workers in a country like Australia. Taiwan (China) may have as many as 200,000 illegal workers, and Malaysia as many as 700,000.

Pressures for movement of labor will increase as the region becomes more integrated through trade in goods and services and movement of capital. The remarkable heterogeneity of East Asia in living standards and factor endowments will make pressures for migration increasingly powerful. Demographic trends in such countries as Japan will lead to declining labor forces within a decade, whereas labor force growth in China and the Philippines will accelerate for some time.

Despite this longer-term potential for labor migration, actual movements of workers are unlikely to be large in the near future because of constraints

cent in 1992, and East Asian low- and middle-income countries increased their share of all FDI (including that by OECD countries) from 4 percent in 1986 to 13 percent in 1992 (table 4.1).

The sharp increase in FDI flows to East Asian low- and middle-income countries was associated with the appreciation of the yen in 1985 and the subsequent strengthening of the Korean and Taiwanese currencies. Malaysia and Thailand were the major beneficiaries. Between 1986 and 1991, FDI inflows to these countries increased sixfold, accounting for about 40 percent of the total for East Asian low- and middle-income countries in 1991. Indonesia attracted about 10 percent of the total FDI inflows, and the Philippines 5 percent. China accounted for more than 60 percent of total FDI inflows in 1986, but its share declined to 39 percent by 1991 as its economy slowed under an austerity program. In 1992 there was a new FDI surge into China—much of it from Hong Kong, Singapore, and Taiwan (China)—resulting in inflows of more than $11 on both demand and supply. On the demand side, it is increasingly recognized that migration does not offer a real solution to short-term macroeconomic problems or to long-term demographic problems of aging populations. In the short term, migrant-related expenditures in a host country create demands for more labor, and the level of migration is seldom large enough to solve labor shortages. In the longer term, the effects of migration on dependency ratios tend to be small and transitory owing to the aging of the migrants. A large and rising future immigration inflow is needed to offset this effect. The European guest-worker system suggests that migrants deprived of basic political and social rights remain a major disadvantaged class and a source of social conflict.

Over the medium term, very few countries—except possibly China and the Philippines—will have any significant excess supply of labor. With rapid growth in incomes and a slowdown of population growth, Malaysia, Thailand, and the East Asian NIEs are more likely to experience labor shortages than surpluses. Migration from these countries to others in the region is likely to be moderate. A major factor in determining permanent migration is expected lifetime earnings in the migrant's own country versus those in the potential destination country. For East Asian countries enjoying rapid growth, the longer-term prospects for factor price equalization through trade and capital movements are bright. This may reduce the attraction of higher current wages in other countries.

So, labor migration is unlikely to do as much as trade and investment in promoting integration in East Asia. The principal policy actions required involve improving the transparency of rules governing migrant labor and relaxing these rules where needed for facilitating the movement of goods, services, and capital.

---

billion. A significant part of these flows (more than 20 percent) is estimated to be recycled funds from China.

The sources of FDI in East Asia are now predominantly intraregional (table 4.2). During 1986–92 about 70 percent of the flows were from East Asia, about 50 percent from NIEs. The share of European and U.S. flows combined was about 20 percent—less than Hong Kong's.

The sectoral composition of FDI is also changing. While earlier investments by OECD countries were often concentrated in resource-related sectors, the NIEs today are investing mainly in manufacturing sectors—particularly electrical machinery, electronics, nonferrous metals, and chemicals. Japanese investments are more dispersed.

The most important determinants of FDI appear to be the policies of recipient and supplier countries, firm-specific attributes that underlie the competitive advantages of transnational corporations, the ability of transnationals to

Despite a recent decline in global FDI flows, East Asian low- and middle-income countries continue to attract large amounts.

TABLE 4.1   NET INFLOW OF FDI TO EAST ASIA

FDI flows	1986	1987	1988	1989	1990	1991	1992
Billions of dollars							
Total	78.8	123.6	151.3	192.4	204.0	158.4	149.9
All developing countries	12.4	14.4	22.0	25.8	31.4	39.6	50.4
East Asia[a]	3.0	3.8	6.5	8.0	9.9	12.5	19.4
Percentage of total							
All developing countries	15.7	11.7	14.5	13.4	15.4	25.0	33.6
East Asia[a]	3.8	3.1	4.3	4.2	4.9	7.9	12.9

a. In this table, East Asia comprises China, Indonesia, Malaysia, the Philippines, and Thailand.
Source: IMF (1993).

gain from internalizing market relationships, and the suitability of recipient countries as locations for foreign production by transnational corporations. Appropriate policies in host countries are necessary for attracting FDI, but perhaps not sufficient for stimulating large inflows (World Bank 1992).

A survey of 173 Japanese investors in manufacturing confirms that the overall economic environment—including market size and the cost of labor and capital goods—is important in determining FDI flows (Kawaguchi 1994; Mody forthcoming).

- FDI policies such as local ownership requirements, restrictions on repatriation of earnings, and requirements on local content (that is, the use of domestic components in production) were serious disincentives to investment.
- Tax incentives were not important.
- Trade policy issues—in particular, high tariffs on parts and components—were obstacles, especially for such technology-intensive sectors as general and electric machinery.

The Impact of Foreign Direct Investment

When developing countries were following import substitution policies, FDI was seen as a way of jumping trade barriers. Under these circumstances, FDI can be welfare-reducing. Today, FDI is increasingly being used to enhance export capabilities. Japanese affiliates in the ASEAN countries, particularly in technology-intensive industries, are strengthening their export capability (table

FDI in East Asia is now primarily intraregional.

TABLE 4.2   FDI INFLOWS TO LOW- AND MIDDLE-INCOME EAST ASIA, BY SOURCE, 1986–92

Source	China		Indonesia		Malaysia		Philippines		Thailand		Total	
	Millions of US$	Percent	Millions of US$	Percent	Millions of US$	Percent	Millions of US$	Percent	Millions of US$	Percent	Millions of US$	Percent
ASEAN	238	0.8	33	0.5	750	5.4	18	0.5	46	0.5	1,085	1.7
Europe	1,316	4.4	1,009	16.1	2,711	19.6	378	11.7	1,108	11.0	6,522	10.3
Japan	3,042	10.2	1,102	17.6	3,065	22.2	855	26.4	3,586	35.6	11,650	18.4
NIES	21,123	70.9	1,573	25.2	4,123	29.8	580	17.9	3,565	35.4	30,964	49.0
United States	2,390	8.0	428	6.8	1,499	10.8	1,193	36.9	1,373	13.6	6,884	10.9
Rest of the world	1,676	5.6	2,105	33.7	1,674	12.1	211	6.5	393	3.9	6,058	9.6
All countries[a]	29,785	100.0	6,250	100.0	13,822	100.0	3,235	100.0	10,071	100.0	63,163	100.0

Note: The totals of arrival inflow data for Indonesia, Malaysia, and the Philippines are derived from IMF (1993). Because the investor country breakdowns of arrival inflow data for these countries are unavailable, those data are calculated by multiplying the totals of arrival by the ratios of approval inflows (in the case of the Philippines, central bank registered inflows). The data for China and Thailand are arrival inflows. The data for Thailand are converted into U.S. dollars by using the year-average exchange rates.

a. Percentages may not total precisely 100.0 because of rounding.

Source: Japan Institute for Overseas Investment (1993); IMF (1993).

Foreign affiliates operating in East Asia are becoming increasingly export-oriented.

TABLE 4.3   EXPORTS OF JAPANESE MANUFACTURING AFFILIATES AS A SHARE OF THEIR
TOTAL SALES, 1986 AND 1992
(percent)

	Location of affiliate	*1986*	*1992*
	Indonesia	3.8	16.5
	Malaysia	48.0	63.0
	Philippines	65.0	54.3
	Thailand	7.9	39.6

Source: MITI (1986, 1992).

4.3). Worldwide analysis of the relationship between FDI and exports does not capture these more recent trends in East Asia, but the relationship is evident in recent developments in Malaysia and Thailand and vital for policymaking in China, Indonesia, the Philippines, and Viet Nam. The role of FDI in promoting growth has been evident in Singapore over the past quarter century, and in Thailand, Malaysia, and China over the past five years.

Singapore.   After a phase of import substitution during 1959–65, the government moved to an export-oriented industrialization strategy with liberal trade policies. As of 1973, the government had introduced more generous investment incentives than those offered by other developing countries, reflecting its choice of FDI as the vehicle for launching industrialization. Foreign companies were allowed complete ownership in almost all industries.

These policy initiatives—combined with a stable macroeconomic environment, human resource development, and able governance—led to a surge of foreign investment, particularly after 1967. Initially, the bulk of investment came from the United States, mostly in petroleum refineries and electronics. Later, political uncertainties in Hong Kong resulted in some textile and garment plants moving to Singapore. These investments generated large increases in employment, industrial output, and exports. The government later attracted FDI to technology-oriented industries and to small and medium-size industries. Manufacturing firms with foreign-majority ownership accounted for 85 percent of exports, about 60 percent of jobs, and two-thirds of value added in 1980, when FDI began to expand in computers, finance, electronics, machinery, printing, and pharmaceuticals.

Thailand.   The Thai government has traditionally had a liberal attitude toward FDI. Thai tax laws and most regulations make no major distinctions between domestic and foreign investment. An important exception is that foreigners are generally not allowed to own land, so they rely on long-term leases. Restrictions apply to the number of foreign technicians and managers who can work in Thailand, and some areas, particularly farming, are closed to foreigners. These are minor restrictions compared with those that many developing countries impose, and they can be circumvented if a foreign firm receives Board of Investment promotion. That promotion gives a company access to imported machinery, parts, and materials without paying significant tariffs, putting it on the same footing as domestic firms. In the early 1980s, this policy was further liberalized for export-oriented FDI in plants that exported more than 50 percent of their output. Foreigners can hold a majority share in promoted investments, and plants that export all their output can be fully owned by foreigners.

In the wake of the Plaza Accord of 1985 and the subsequent appreciation of the yen and other East Asian currencies, FDI surged from around $270 million a year in the first half of the 1980s to nearly $1.5 billion a year during 1987–91 (table 4.4). This increase contributed to a doubling of Thailand's annual GDP growth rate to nearly 11 percent, exceeding even Korea's growth rate when Korea was at a comparable level of per capita income. Merchandise exports more than tripled, rising from around $8.8 billion in 1986 to over $28 billion by 1991. The average export propensity of foreign firms rose from 10 percent in 1971 to 33 percent in 1984 and to more than 50 percent by 1988. More than half of Thailand's total exports are manufactured goods such as electrical ap-

Malaysia and Thailand are the FDI-led miracles in East Asia.

TABLE 4.4   SELECTED ECONOMIC INDICATORS FOR MALAYSIA AND THAILAND

Indicator	Malaysia		Thailand	
	1981–86	1987–91	1981–86	1987–91
Average annual GDP growth (percent)	4.5	8.4	5.5	10.7
Ratio of gross domestic investment to GDP (average percentage)	32.9	29.3	24.3	32.2
Merchandise exports, end-year (billions of dollars)	13.8	34.3	8.8	28.3
Average annual growth of exports (percent)	9.1	13.2	11.2	19.9
Average annual FDI flows (millions of dollars)	984	1,843	274	1,428[a]

a. Data are for 1988–91.
Source: World Bank data.

pliances, machinery, transportation parts, and chemicals, produced mostly by foreign investors.

During the late 1980s, Japanese component makers came to Thailand, mainly to assist the Japanese multinationals with which they were affiliated at home. Now, however, Japanese multinationals are increasingly using Thai sources to procure simpler plastic and metal parts, while helping local suppliers upgrade their quality. Subcontracting is becoming an effective avenue for local manufacturers to assimilate foreign technology. Several Japanese joint ventures associated with carmakers have begun to export as well as to supply the local market with Thai-made molds and dies. Japanese makers have begun to use Thailand as a base for integrating their automobile production in Asia—for example, Mitsubishi, Nissan, and Toyota are arranging a network to source more parts from ASEAN countries.

In the textile industry, Japanese manufacturers—such as Kuravo Company and Toyo Rayon Company—were the only exporters from Thailand during the 1970s. Since then, Japanese firms have withdrawn, and local textile firms have transformed themselves into exporters by building on the business contacts and technology learned from Japanese firms.

Most impressive is Thailand's electrical and electronics industry. Japanese producers appear to have selected Thailand as a key offshore production base in their global networks, manufacturing standard products there for export to Japan and other parts of the world. Electronics and electrical industries have become Thailand's leading export sector, with exports of $4.6 billion, or 16.5 percent of all exports, in 1991.

Malaysia.   The story of FDI-assisted development in Malaysia is equally impressive. As in Singapore, foreign affiliates were important in Malaysia's development even before the investment boom began in 1985. At that time, foreign firms accounted for 38 percent of total registered capital in Malaysian manufacturing, and exports by foreign firms accounted for a similar proportion of total manufacturing exports. With the post–Plaza Accord appreciation of the yen, FDI in Malaysia more than doubled within five years. In 1992, FDI flows amounted to more than $4 billion, the highest in the developing world on a per capita basis. This investment boom has been associated with a doubling of growth in GDP, from around 4.5 percent a year in the first half of the 1980s to about 8.4 percent in the second half (table 4.4). Exports tripled within five years, reaching $34 billion in 1991—higher on a per capita basis than Korea's at a similar stage of development.

Whereas Japan and the United States dominated FDI in the 1970s, the NIES are now making important contributions. Taiwan (China), for example, accounted for 36 percent of approved FDI in 1990, surpassing Japan. Many Taiwanese investors are setting up small and medium-size enterprises in Malaysia, as are other NIEs. Eighty-two percent of foreign projects in 1988–89 exported more than half their output (compared with 24 percent of such projects in 1984–85), and 74 percent exported more than four-fifths. Since many of these new enterprises manufacture components, they increased both intraindustry and intraregional links.

In the electrical and electronics industry, which accounted for 57 percent of total manufactured exports in 1990, foreign investment has been especially significant (box 4.2). Matsushita is the largest Japanese investor in Malaysia, and its sixteen consumer electronics and components companies there represent the company's largest foreign operation in Asia. Matsushita has made Malaysia its chief export base for room air-conditioners, supplying 10 to 15 percent of the world market from two Malaysian factories. Most of these products go to China, Japan, and the United States.

China. The latest example of FDI-led export and technology development in East Asia is China. Starting at a low level in the mid-1980s, FDI has since soared. While accurate figures are difficult to obtain, it is estimated that foreign investment commitments in China amounted to $35 billion in 1992, more than the total for the preceding ten years. Disbursed investment in China is estimated at around $9 billion for 1992 and over $20 billion in 1993—about eleven times that in 1986.[6] These flows have been associated largely with textile and footwear exports from China. Hong Kong firms now employ more people in China—about 2 million—than they do in Hong Kong. Taiwanese and U.S. firms have also been increasing their stake, helping to develop local technology.

Nike, an international shoe producer and distributor, provides an interesting example of how FDI can develop technological capability. In the mid-1980s Nike attempted to produce low-end shoes in China, but because the quality was unacceptable, the company adopted a different strategy for exploiting production-cost advantages. It negotiated with Taiwanese producers, who agreed to locate production supervisors at factories in Fujian province, adjacent to Taiwan (China). The quality of production improved greatly, and today China is the largest exporter of shoes to the United States—ahead of Taiwan (China) in volume though not in value.

A Better Alternative to Fostering Industries

Developing technological capability and fostering infant industries have been important aspects of development policies since World War II. The initial approach was to establish import protection for infant industries, supported by

BOX 4.2 THE ELECTRONICS INDUSTRY IN MALAYSIA

The electronics industry accounts for the largest share of manufacturing output, value added, exports, and employment in Malaysia. During 1981–88, its output expanded from $3.6 billion to $9.4 billion, an average increase of almost 15 percent a year. By 1987, electronics exports were Malaysia's top revenue earner, contributing $6.9 billion to the national accounts. Most of this was due to the well-established multinational semiconductor firms. Malaysia is now the world's leading exporter of semiconductors and the third largest producer after Japan and the United States, with one of the largest installed semiconductor assembly capacities in the world. The total electronics production of Malaysia in 1987 was $2 billion, or 0.9 percent of the world's total.

The industry gained a foothold in 1967, when a Japanese multinational set up a consumer electronics plant in Malaysia to take advantage of the domestic market. In 1971 the semiconductor business was started when an American multinational invested in Malaysia. Many other multinationals did the same, following active government promotion of foreign investment to develop labor-intensive industries. Initially feared to be a "footloose" industry associated with assembly-type operations in free trade or export processing zones, electronics has developed into a major area of high-technology investment and development.

The Investment Incentives Act of 1968 and the establishment of free trade zones in 1972 encouraged the influx of foreign companies into the electronics industry. Beyond the general foreign investment incentives, however, the electronics industry was singled out. In the early 1970s, as the U.S. semiconductor makers were relocating their labor-intensive assembly operations to developing countries, Malaysia's Federal Industrial Development Authority coordinated specific investment missions to attract their attention. Later, as U.S. investment in Malaysia declined during the recession of the mid-1980s, the Authority aimed its efforts at the surrounding NIEs. These economies, especially Taiwan (China), began to move their plants to Southeast Asian countries because of rising labor costs and currency appreciations at home. Their reliance on small and medium-

government assistance for credit, procurement, and technological support. Results were mixed. While some countries had success with infant-industry protection, the majority found themselves saddled with inefficient industries supported by unearned "rents" that roiled the political and social atmosphere. An emerging alternative is FDI-led industry development within the context of relatively open trade regimes. The development of the computer industry in East Asia shows the gains from being open to trade and investment, while the auto size enterprises and component industries fits well into Malaysia's entrenched electronics industry and has had a significant impact on the boom.

The electronics industry is characterized by rapid technological change that necessitates continual investment in facilities and equipment, technology and skills transfer, and development of ancillary industries. The industry's value added expanded by 28 percent in real terms between 1973 and 1981 and by 10 percent between 1981 and 1988. Its contribution to GDP increased steadily from 2.1 percent in 1981 to 3.0 percent in 1988. Correspondingly, its share of manufactured exports rose from 48 percent to 56 percent. The industry's employment increased from 16 to 22 percent of total manufacturing employment. Among the key reasons for this success were the wealth of available labor and the efficient use of that labor.

Over the past two decades, continuing investments by multinationals have transformed the industry from a labor-intensive operation in the early 1970s to a capital- and technology-intensive operation today. The investments have gone into upgrading equipment, expanding production facilities, developing backward and forward integration, establishing local research and development capability, and improving quality. They have also resulted in a gradual expansion into areas of higher technology: automated assembly equipment, computer-aided manufacturing, device testing, robotics, and computer-aided design. Consequently, there has been some success in the transfer of skills and technology. Many multinationals have established formal apprenticeship programs for precision-tool engineering, local and overseas scholarships, and skills development courses. And the equipment, materials, and infrastructural support required by the electronics sector have resulted in the creation of ancillary industries.

The Penang Skills Development Center is a good example of the forward thinking that has propelled the industry. A public and private sector joint venture, the Center was given tax-exempt status, and much of its equipment is donated by the industry. It provides training courses not just to its members but to the entire manufacturing sector, and it has emerged as one of the leading training institutes in the country.

Source: Salleh and Meyanathan (1993).

---

mobile industry shows both the problems of protection and the gains of openness.

The Computer Industry

Computer manufacturing is often seen as an archetype of a technology-intensive industry well suited to infant-industry protection. Korea and Taiwan

(China) used protection to encourage their domestic computer industries. But in the past five years, both have cut tariffs to near zero and reduced quantitative restrictions on most products. China and Thailand have also lowered duties affecting the computer industry. In general, tariff rates in the East Asian NIEs are now comparable to those in the United States.

Most East Asian economies have encouraged FDI flows, with particular emphasis on technology transfer. Singapore offers a tax incentive known as "pioneer status" to foreign or domestic companies that carry out high-technology research and development and make other investments in designated high-technology industries. Taiwan (China) gives tax credits of 5 to 20 percent to companies that invest in automated production equipment, technology, or research and development (R&D). China, Indonesia, Malaysia, and Thailand all offer free trade zones, and Malaysia has a linkage policy to strengthen the bonds between foreign subsidiaries and local supporting industry, with technology transfers as a crucial element.

The region experienced a boom in computer products in the 1980s. Worldwide computer price wars pushed U.S. and Japanese makers to look to the NIEs as cost-effective production centers, and similar forces are now moving investment and production from the NIEs to other East Asian economies. In Hong Kong, Singapore, and Taiwan (China), land and labor are in short supply. But China, Indonesia, and Malaysia have ample supplies of both, and they have established free trade zones to encourage investment. Singapore is encouraging offshore production of labor-intensive products as part of an economic plan to increase skilled employment and value added. The situation is similar in Hong Kong, where many computer parts firms rely on relatively inexpensive labor in the Shenzen special economic zone across the Chinese border for assembly and finishing, while design and packaging are done in Hong Kong. Most components produced in these operations are shipped to the parent company for incorporation into finished products.

Growing technological expertise in East Asia is increasing production capabilities so that some components no longer have to be imported. Over the past twenty years, Singapore has upgraded its product and process technology to move from making lower-end computer products to higher-end hard disk drives. At the same time, lower technology disk-drive production was moved to Malaysia and Thailand.

This process is achieving regional integration to an extent that earlier industrial strategies did not. Throughout the region, the level of computer technology and production is increasing, and East Asian markets for computer equipment are growing at 20 to 30 percent a year, with domestic and foreign-owned producers in East Asia supplying an increasing share of these markets. Investment patterns in the region also contribute to intraregional trade. As producers set up operations in more than one East Asian country, intracompany transfers augment regional trade. Sourcing from regional suppliers allows firms to rely on just-in-time inventory and to source from several suppliers, switching when components are difficult to obtain or prices change. Intraregional trade, growing much faster than external trade, now accounts for 25 percent of NIE trade in computers.

The Automotive Industry

Most East Asian economies are entering a phase of economic development in which the demand for automobiles is likely to grow rapidly. Between 1987 and 1991, sales of automobiles in developing East Asia grew by about 8 percent a year, reaching 3 million units. Annual sales could reach about 7 million units by 2000, accounting for more than 7 percent of GDP in these economies. Until recently, OECD countries accounted for about 75 percent of worldwide automotive production and sales. In recent years, sales in OECD markets have been stagnant or declining, leading to huge excess manufacturing capacity and large losses for major producers. European, Japanese, and U.S. automakers need to find ways of cutting costs by outsourcing parts and components.

The Japanese have perfected the technique of saving on inventories and fixed costs by developing a domestic supply chain for various parts within a framework of tight controls on quality and timeliness of delivery. This approach is now being extended beyond national borders, bringing into the automobile industry the global "borderless factory" that already characterizes computer production.

Developing East Asia could become a significant partner in this global industry, whose annual output may exceed $1 trillion by 2000. Within a decade, East Asia could become a major supplier of parts and components, and eventually of assembled vehicles, much as it has for toys, textiles, and footwear and much as it is now doing for electronics.

But the present policies of most East Asian countries are not geared to exploiting these opportunities. They have very high import protection, selective import bans, high local-content requirements, mandatory use of locally produced auto parts, foreign exchange–earning requirements, and restrictions on foreign equity holdings. Because Indonesia has highly restrictive trade and investment regimes in the automotive sector, approximately 80 percent of the larger auto parts firms are locally owned, though they often have technical agreements with foreign firms.

Unless quick action is taken, these trade protection regimes are likely to solidify, creating huge rents that go largely to major domestic suppliers and to foreign investors. In China, ex-factory prices of passenger cars have been 100 to

200 percent higher than the border price (before duties), although prices are lower for trucks. For most other countries with tariff rates of up to 200 percent, effective protection rates on value added have been equally enormous. A conservative estimate suggests that the rent on local production in East Asia is around $5,000 per vehicle—equivalent to $15 billion a year of extra costs to consumers.

It is tempting to assume that the rationale for protecting auto industries is to follow in the footsteps of Japan and Korea. In the early phase of its industrial development, Japan protected automotive production, although at a much lower level of protection (tariffs of about 35 percent) than most East Asian countries have today. Korean protection levels, also lower, have come down in recent years. The world has changed since the days when Japan and Korea were building their automotive industries through indigenous technology and domestic financing. In today's global market for technology, capital, and management, newcomers can develop these industries better through FDI than through protection. Effective outsourcing of parts by major OECD producers will be possible only if they can be assured of quality and delivery schedules, and this can only be helped by more liberal trade and FDI flows.

There are, of course, many differences between the computer industry and the automobile industry. An investment of around $200 million is typically required for the assembly of knocked-down automobile kits, while fully integrated manufacturing requires an investment of around $1.5 billion. Start-up costs are much smaller for personal computer products. An automotive vehicle requires some 10,000 parts, compared with a few hundred for a personal computer. Still, the restructuring of production patterns by European and U.S. automakers and the further movement of Japanese production offshore in response to the yen's continuing appreciation provide opportunities for an export-oriented FDI policy in East Asia.

The Political Economy of Trade and Investment

FDI, instead of being dominated by large multinationals, is oriented toward small and medium-size enterprises as well. These smaller firms are not seen as a threat to national sovereignty, and their procurement and production decisions are influenced more by economic considerations than by global corporate strategies. Instead of exploiting the economic rents created by import substitution, foreign investors are geared increasingly to promote exports, especially textiles, footwear, electronics, and electrical products. In 1992 the ratio of exports to total sales of Japanese affiliates in manufacturing was 45 percent in Asia, compared with 23 percent in Latin America.

The trade-FDI link in East Asia is often illustrated by the "flying geese" hypothesis, according to which the dispersion of technology that influences trade patterns is transmitted through FDI from the lead country to follower countries (Akamatsu 1960). Lead-country firms, to combine their technological advantage with the lower factor costs in follower countries, move production of "second-tier" products offshore. The combination of foreign capital and cheaper production costs makes the follower country's products more competitive in world markets, so exports rise. Japan is usually regarded as the lead country, followed by the early NIEs, which in turn have been followed by Malaysia, Thailand, and more recently, China. In FDI-led infant-industry development, private investors—motivated by profit rather than bureaucratic process—are proving to be more effective instruments of training and technology transfer than are bureaucrats using public funds. Furthermore, the distribution of production according to comparative advantage and the ability of host countries to absorb technology is being helped by FDI flows within an increasingly open trading system.

The link between FDI and exports is changing the political economy of protectionism. International investors are creating a pressure group for trade liberalization that will enable them to distribute production among different national units of their borderless factories. Surveys undertaken for this report confirm that timely availability of parts and components is important in attracting FDI and that the process is facilitated by a liberal trade regime (Kawaguchi 1994; Mody forthcoming). Foreign producers also pressure host country governments to relax import restrictions, often contributing to a more open trade regime.

Such pressures for trade liberalization in East Asia have so far operated case by case. As things stand, government officials and political leaders liberalize trade only for particular items. This process, costly in both bureaucratic and political terms, is becoming difficult to manage as the scope for FDI expands into new and unpredictable areas.

There is clearly a virtuous circle for FDI and trade. Trade liberalization attracts FDI, which contributes to export growth, which in turn creates pressure for further trade liberalization. The changing external resource position of many East Asian developing countries further strengthens the circle. Some countries, such as Indonesia and the Philippines, previously relied heavily on borrowings by the public sector. Debt servicing has assumed significant proportions, and the net transfer of resources through public sector borrowing is becoming increasingly small. FDI provides an attractive alternative to such flows because it does not create fixed-debt obligations. Related outflows are tied to the profits from investments, in turn linked to the host country's competitiveness. And FDI flows, if export-oriented, will earn foreign exchange to help service external debt.

FDI can nevertheless have adverse effects on a host country's balance of payments or on the development of its production capabilities. In the short run, imports of capital goods associated with FDI can increase the current account deficit, though this usually is more than offset by the impact of the FDI inflows on the capital account. In the longer run, the repatriation of capital, profits, and management fees by foreign investors could equal—or exceed—the repayment of principal and interest on foreign loans.

In some cases, multinational corporations could also resort to exclusive and expensive purchases through intrafirm transactions, and they could use such practices as "transfer pricing" of capital goods, intermediates, and components to minimize taxes or to shift profits. Multinationals with dominant market positions might obtain investment agreements to restrict technology diffusion, innovations in process, and the destination or volume of exports to third-country markets where they have subsidiaries. All this implies a need for a transparent system of FDI promotion and for careful monitoring of corporate behavior.

In East Asia the benefits of FDI have outweighed the costs. One key factor that made this possible was the export orientation (rather than import-substitution orientation) of the FDI in manufacturing, particularly in Malaysia and Thailand. The pressures for efficiency and competitiveness have helped in local sourcing of inputs when economically rational. The foreign exchange earnings have also helped alleviate the debt servicing burden and enabled Malaysia and Thailand to allow freer repatriation of profits.

Prospects for Foreign Direct Investment in the 1990s

During the 1990s, the pool of investable resources that can be attracted to low- and middle-income East Asian countries is likely to grow. Despite efforts to reduce the trade surplus, Japan's substantial current account surpluses are likely to continue during the 1990s. The percentage of overseas production in Japanese manufacturing is 6 percent, compared with 23 percent for the United States and 17 percent for Germany. The yen's appreciation, while reducing the trade surplus somewhat, could generate another wave of Japanese investments abroad.

East Asian economies would be the major beneficiary. The NIEs have accumulated large foreign exchange balances and continue to run current account surpluses. Most are having to cope with rising labor costs at home and are looking for opportunities to outsource production. FDI from NIEs and some ASEAN countries is becoming increasingly important for East Asian low- and middle-income countries. Although the United States is likely to be preoccupied with investments in Latin America, there are some areas—especially electronics, chemicals, and automobiles—for which East Asia could prove an attractive investment destination. According to capital expenditure planning in 1993, majority-owned affiliates of U.S. companies in developing East Asia expect their investments in the region to rise substantially in the coming years.

In a climate of financial stringency, Japanese companies are becoming more concerned with profitability than with market share. Operating profit rates on sales of Japanese affiliates in Asia have been significantly higher than those in Europe and the United States (table 4.5). Many of Japan's larger corporations, which earlier moved to North America and Europe to overcome protectionism, are now looking to Asian markets.

A doubling of total FDI to developing East Asia from the baseline projections is realistic so long as the policy framework is favorable in both home and host countries. China is a very strong candidate for increased FDI flows—from overseas Chinese investors in Hong Kong, Korea, Singapore, Taiwan (China), and ASEAN and from industrial countries. In addition to production cost advantages, China offers a huge domestic market and significant possibilities for exports. FDI flows to China, discounting today's enthusiasm, can be expected to double between 1993 and 2000 (box 4.3). Indonesia is another promising area for FDI inflows, as the country speeds the liberalization of its policies. Malaysia and Thailand can also continue to be attractive destinations by containing the rise in business costs and improving infrastructure. And Viet Nam is emerging as a strong candidate for FDI. The outlook for the Philippines and other island economies will improve as they strengthen their policies.

Manufacturing can be expected to dominate FDI flows, with textiles, footwear, and electronics remaining the favored industries as countries advance in "flying geese" formation. Infrastructure investment is also expanding (box 4.4).

Japanese companies in Asia, unlike their counterparts in Europe and North America, are improving their profitability.

TABLE 4.5   OPERATING PROFIT RATES ON SALES BY LOCAL AFFILIATES
OF JAPANESE COMPANIES
(percentage of sales revenue)

Location of Japanese affiliate	FY 86	FY 87	FY 88	FY 89	FY 90	FY 91
Asia	1.2	2.5	3.2	2.0	3.0	3.3
Europe	1.2	1.2	1.2	0.8	1.1	0.0
North America	0.3	0.1	0.6	0.5	20.1	20.6

Source: MITI (1993).

The rapidly growing economic activities in China, Hong Kong, and Taiwan (China) are turning this area into a fourth growth pole of the world economy. The output of this area, measured in standard international prices, makes it the world's second largest economy behind the United States. Its imports are two-thirds as large as Japan's and could be greater a decade from now. Among the world's major economies, China, Hong Kong, and Taiwan (China) together are the fastest-growing, averaging 7 percent per year since 1962 and expected to do even better in the near future.

Like other East Asian economies, these three benefit from strong and intensifying international economic linkages. Hong Kong and Taiwan (China) have long been aggressively outward-oriented, and China's recent approach has also stressed this strategy. Between 1980 and 1990, China's trade-to-GDP ratio increased from 13 percent to 39 percent, and between 1979 and 1992 China received $35 billion in foreign direct investment.

This remarkable transformation has been engineered in part by vigorous entrepreneurship from Hong Kong and Taiwan (China). The extent of integration is quite extraordinary. About 19 percent of all Chinese exports—primarily processed goods—are classified in Section 9 of the Standard International Trade Classification (SITC). An additional 20 percent of Chinese exports are produced by foreign or joint venture companies, 60 percent of which are from Hong Kong. Still another large share goes through Hong Kong intermediaries. More than 70 percent of Hong Kong's exports are now reexports of products made in China. Hong Kong entrepreneurs are estimated to own 20,000 Chinese enterprises and employ 2 million Chinese workers. Taiwan

Reform of Investment Regimes

The East Asian experience points to the huge gains from the integrated liberalization of trade and investment. Most East Asian countries are loosening restrictions on FDI—concerning sector allocation, ownership, local employment, and performance requirements on local content and export obligation—as well as removing restrictions on capital transfer. But many restrictive elements need to be relaxed (table 4.6) and proper regulations strengthened. Many countries need more transparent regulatory frameworks that can help to improve the *quality* of FDI. For these reasons, FDI policies in East Asia merit further reform.

Special FDI incentives, such as tax concessions, often fail to attract additional investment and are generally self-defeating. Moreover, certain tax incentives for FDI may simply transfer funds from the host country to the home country treasury, without benefiting foreign investors. A low overall tax regime (low corporate tax rate on a broad base) is the best strategy for encouraging FDI. Also, the tax regime

(China) is close behind, with an estimated investment of $15 billion in 7,000 firms. China has reciprocated by investing $12 billion in Hong Kong.

These links make the area a truly formidable competitor. With a huge market, low wages, and considerable marketing and production know-how, it is a major force in world manufacturing. A massive reorganization of production is under way as manufacturing operations are shifted from Hong Kong and Taiwan (China) to China. Between 1980 and 1990, the share of manufacturing in Hong Kong's GDP fell from 24 to 17 percent, and similar trends are now emerging in Taiwan (China). One result of this was that Hong Kong and Taiwan (China)'s trade surplus with the United States declined by $15 billion between 1987 and 1992. But China's surplus increased by $15 billion, leaving the area's overall surplus unchanged at $28 billion. To be sure, these flows are extremely difficult to measure. For example, U.S. Customs reported $26 billion in imports from China in 1992, but Chinese statistics showed only $9 billion in exports to the United States. The balance presumably passed through Hong Kong as reexports.

The regional implications are just beginning to be felt. The area's rapid growth could spill over to other economies in East Asia, many of which export 3 percent or more of their GDP to the area. Its immense investment requirements and increasingly market-oriented policies are creating exceptional opportunities for foreign investment. And the export growth in these economies generates powerful pressures for adjustments elsewhere, in critical markets such as the United States and in competing exporting countries, such as the NIES and the ASEAN countries.

---

in source countries is at least as important as that in the recipient country in influencing decisions to locate investments.

Even more important than special FDI policies are general policies affecting trade, labor markets, credit and fiscal policies, and the development of human resources, infrastructure, the environment, and supporting industries—issues often addressed in adjustment programs. These policies remain vital because the performance of host countries will be judged by the market and by private investors, not by official agencies.

Trade and investment liberalization by the East Asian countries would benefit the liberalizing countries as well as their trading partners. And the more advanced countries of East Asia, Australia, North America, and elsewhere should gain from FDI flows that sustain trade liberalization in the region.

Japan has several measures to support Japanese investors abroad, such as the foreign investment–loss reserve system, the exemption from international double taxation, the long-term loans from the Japan Export-Import Bank and

In most developing countries, infrastructure activities—building, maintaining, and operating power, transportation, and communication facilities—have traditionally been in the public domain. With the rapid economic growth in East Asian countries, infrastructural facilities are failing to keep up with demand. Moreover, the resources needed to meet these requirements are enormous—an estimated $1 trillion to $1.5 trillion during the 1990s. Public agencies responsible for infrastructure are finding it difficult to raise such vast sums. The resource shortage, combined with the cost advantages of the private sector, is increasing interest in the role of the private sector in developing infrastructure.

Interestingly, this trend was started by a socialist economy in transition, when China privatized the construction of the Hong Kong–Shensun Highway and Shijiao Power Plant. There are now more than a dozen such infrastructure projects in East Asian countries covering power, telecommunications, and roads. Financing, physical construction, and initial operation are entrusted to the private investor, usually a consortium of specialized firms, foreign or local, that enter into an agreement with the local authority. A number of variations have developed, such as build, operate, and transfer; build, own, and operate; build, transfer, and operate; and build, lease, and operate. Private parties may also invest in the rehabilitation of deficiently maintained facilities, making agreements to rehabilitate, operate, and transfer; rehabilitate, own, and operate; rehabilitate, transfer, and operate; or rehabilitate, lease, and operate.

In a build-operate-transfer contract, two factors are expected to reduce the project cost and improve effi-

the Small Business Finance Corporation, and the overseas investment guarantees by the Ministry of International Trade and Industry (MITI). MITI has guidelines for overseas operations to encourage Japanese corporations to promote technology transfer and local R&D activity, to establish good labor relations and help in human development, and to concern themselves fully with local environmental problems. Japan is also expanding its measures to assist small and medium-size enterprises in investing abroad.

The source countries benefit from the income generation from the FDI flows. There is also likely to be a supply-side response to the extent that the additional FDI flows are associated with policies that increase the level and efficiency of overall investments. In the case of Japan and other East Asian suppliers of FDI, this report envisages improved overall investments under a package of trade and investment liberalization. (Though not considered in this report, similar effects can result in other source countries, too.)

ciency. One is the reduction of interfacing problems in implementation. Parties to separate but interrelated contracts spend much of their time and resources positioning themselves on favorable legal grounds. In a well-defined build-operate-transfer (or build-own-operate) project, the owner, contractor, and operator are all the same party, with no interest in delaying the project. Second, any financial outlay ultimately has to be justified through operation and profit. Over-specification and delayed procurement are likely to be prevented. Similarly, the builder-operator has a strong incentive to practice strict quality control.

Privatizing infrastructure is not enough for success. The public authority has to have a firm commitment and active support for the approach in planning the project, concluding the agreement, and making implementation adjustments. A loosely defined project will suffer from conflicts of interest between the sponsor and the owner, as in the light-rail transit project in Manila and the Kumagai Urban Expressway project in Bangkok. Of particular importance is the determination to prevent cost overruns caused by indecision.

The project sponsor also needs to adapt to new situations. The sponsor is most likely to have a fast-track advantage. Likewise, the contractor of the sponsorship will enjoy larger responsibility as well as broader authority to execute the project. Tight site management, strict quality and cost control, and timely decisions can maximize the inherent merit of privatization. A small discrepancy in the beginning can produce a major financial mismatch afterward, in turn leading to disputes among the parties concerned. The project sponsor—the main agent of the action—must redefine its role as the chief risk-taker.

A consultative mechanism might be useful in the process of reforming FDI policies and increasing the quantity *and* quality of FDI. The first step could be a seminar to discuss specific policy areas, bringing together officials of major source and host countries and representatives of their business communities.

Despite great progress, investment reform is an unfinished agenda in East Asia.

TABLE 4.6 IMPEDIMENTS TO FDI IN SIX EAST ASIAN COUNTRIES

Areas of concern	China	Indonesia	Malaysia	Philippines	Thailand	Viet Nam
Barriers to entry	General negative clause. Certain sectors (services and others) are closed.	General negative clause. Certain subsectors are closed.	No negative clause. Mass media are closed.	No negative clause. Certain sectors (services and others) are closed.	No general negative clause. Certain sectors (services and others) are closed.	No negative clause. No sectors are closed.
Full foreign ownership requirements	Full ownership allowed under restricted conditions, such as those relating to technology level and export ratio.	Full ownership allowed for firms that export all output, firms with more than $50 million of investment, and other designated locations. Obligation for localization.	Full ownership allowed for firms that export more than 80% of output in large projects or more than 50% of output in other specific projects.	Full ownership allowed in designated sectors.	Full ownership allowed in firms that export more than 80% of output and in designated sectors/locations. Obligation for localization.	Full ownership discouraged in sectors dominated by state enterprises.

	Local content required on a case-by-case basis. Export requirement a condition.	Certain import of raw materials and intermediate goods restricted to firms that export more than 65% of output. Export requirement a condition for investing in certain sectors and for obtaining incentives and exemption of import restrictions.	Local content required in certain sectors and for tax incentives and export credits. Export requirement a condition for issuing a certain share of foreign equity and for obtaining incentives.	Export requirement a condition for obtaining incentives.	Local content required in certain sectors. Export requirement a condition for issuing a certain share of foreign equity and for obtaining incentives.	No local content requirement. Export requirement a condition for obtaining incentives.
Local content and performance requirements						
Transfer of profits and convertibility	Restrictions apply. Foreign exchange balancing is required.	No restrictions.	No restrictions.	No restrictions.	No restrictions.	Restrictions apply. Foreign exchange balancing is required.

Note: This tables does not necessarily reflect recent changes.
Source: Japan Institute for Overseas Investment (1993).

Options for Trade Liberalization

EAST Asia's development momentum continues to depend on the vigorous expansion of international trade and investment. Unilateral MFN-type liberalizations adopted by several East Asian countries in the past have generated great progress. The completion of the Uruguay Round has set the stage for much greater progress toward global liberalization. There are several options for East Asia and others to liberalize further by rolling back protectionist barriers. Should East Asia's liberalization be unilateral, regional, or both? If regional, should it be discriminatory or nondiscriminatory?

Reforms of Trade Regimes

The main reason for liberalizing trade is to improve welfare in the liberalizing country. The familiar arguments for openness—the static and dynamic gains from trade—have been strengthened in recent years by the growth of FDI and the globalization of corporate strategies. To attract multinational companies and state-of-the-art technology, countries must offer an economic environment as free as possible from import barriers, regulations, taxes, and other interventions.

The main arguments for protection are to support infant industries and, for large countries, to improve the terms of trade. But governments find it hard to pick the right infant industries, the cost of mistakes is high, and "beggar thy neighbor" policies do not pay in the long term. Costly experiences with protection elsewhere and the East Asia region's beneficial results from liberalization explain why even the more interventionist East Asian economies have opted to liberalize.

The region's liberalization agenda is unfinished. In developing a unilateral program, each country tends to ignore the benefits that accrue to its trade partners. If these externalities are highlighted in mutual discussions, it may be possible to achieve greater openness even if a country's liberalization is limited by the desire to nurture infant industries, by terms-of-trade goals, by political constraints, or by other factors.

Multilateral liberalization is difficult, however. MFN clauses are nondiscriminatory and introduce free-rider problems into the negotiating process, as each country seeks to benefit from the concessions of others without offering significant concessions of its own. To minimize free riding, the results of early GATT negotiations were not finalized until each country agreed to the whole package. That gave participants a chance to exert pressure on countries reluctant to make reciprocal offers. Later GATT rounds, in an effort to elicit equal concessions, focused on formula tariff cuts rather than line-by-line negotiations. This approach produced reasonably large tariff cuts but could not be easily carried over to quantitative restrictions and other new issues.

One way to solve the free-rider problem is to limit concessions to signatories. With such discriminatory strategies, countries might be able to extract relatively large reciprocal concessions as a price for participation. The efficacy of this approach is implicitly recognized in Article XXIV of the GATT, which authorizes free trade areas under certain limitations. Preferential trade agreements do not necessarily increase global welfare, however, or even the welfare of signatory countries. By diverting trade from efficient outside partners to inefficient inside partners, preferential agreements can harm excluded trade partners and even included partners (box 5.1). To increase welfare, a preferential area must create more trade than it diverts.

Preferential agreements can increase welfare when countries are members of natural blocs or where intrabloc transport costs are low but external transport costs are high. Preferential agreements also benefit large blocs when countries are diverse enough to specialize efficiently, thereby achieving most of the benefits of global free trade. In addition, preferential blocs can increase welfare by making their producers efficient when scale economies are important. Even if inside producers have higher costs than outside producers initially, the large market of a bloc can eventually help inside producers reduce costs.

The case for or against preferential agreements cannot be decided on theoretical grounds. Experience, however, is equally inconclusive. The Central American Common Market and the European Union created substantial trade with little trade diversion. The Latin American Free Trade Area, by contrast, had substantial trade diversion with little trade creation. Most preferential trading blocs accomplished little, neither creating nor diverting much trade.

BOX 5.1   TRADE CREATION AND TRADE DIVERSION

Suppose that country *A*, previously a nondiscriminatory MFN trader, forms a discriminatory free trade area with country *B*. Products from *B* will enter *A* duty-free, while products from third countries such as *C* will continue to be burdened by a tariff. If partner *B* is the low-cost supplier of a given product, the free trade area may *create* additional trade at the expense of *A*'s inefficient producers. But if *C* is the low-cost supplier, *A* can *divert* its trade to *B*, whose products appear less expensive than *C*'s because they are free of tariffs. While trade creation increases national and global welfare, trade diversion reduces welfare. A free trade area can thus be beneficial or harmful, depending on whether its economic configuration favors trade creation or diversion.

The relative magnitudes of trade creation and diversion can be identi-fied. In the figure, DD' and SS' represent *A*'s demand and supply of a product. Before the existence of the free trade area, *A* imports from *C*, which is assumed to be the low-cost supplier, at a price of, say, $200. With a 50 percent tariff, the price in *A*'s market is $300. After the free trade area comes into being, *A* switches its imports to *B*, because *B*'s price at $220 is lower than *C*'s price of $200 plus the $100 tariff. Trade is created as *A*'s consumption increases by 50 units and as *A*'s inefficient home pro-duction declines by 60 units. But 50 units of trade are diverted from *C* to *B*. The gains from trade creation are measured by areas 3 and 4, and the loss from trade diversion by area 1. Area 2 is neither gained nor lost; it helps *A*'s consumers but reduces *A*'s tariff revenue. The free trade area benefits *A* if the sum of areas 3 and 4 is greater than that of area 1.

A free trade area tends to be welfare-improving if it includes low-

---

What kinds of blocs create or divert trade? A bloc probably is trade-creating if it had intense trading relationships before the preferences were intro-duced, indicating that its members are efficient suppliers of each other's re-quirements. High initial levels of protection also favor trade creation, because liberalization inside the bloc will tend to eliminate inefficient home industries. Large blocs are more likely to be trade-creating than small blocs, since they probably include efficient producers of most of the required commodities. Such criteria are easier to list in theory than to apply in practice. For example, early predictions were pessimistic about the European Community (the forerunner of the EU) because its members had similar resource endowments. Yet it expanded trade, in part because it created considerable intraindustry trade based on econ-omies of scale.

cost (that is, internationally competitive) suppliers for each of the area's major import requirements. Ideally, a free trade area consists of countries that are already intense trading partners under MFN rules and that have diverse comparative advantages. Sectors with large economies of scale also benefit under a free trade agreement if the producers in these sectors cannot reach economical output levels because of protection in world markets.

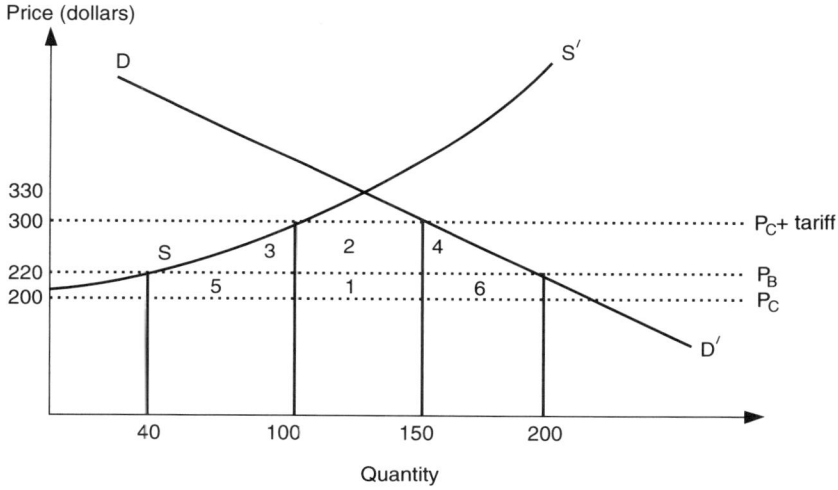

East Asia's Policy Framework

The East Asia region's trade regime includes one formal trading arrangement (the ASEAN Free Trade Area, or AFTA), an inclusive intergovernmental forum (Asia Pacific Economic Cooperation, or APEC), and various formal and informal subregional groupings. An additional group, the East Asian Economic Group (EAEG), has been recast as a consultative caucus. These frameworks could provide mechanisms for implementing regional trade and investment initiatives.

Regional Institutions

The Association of Southeast Asian Nations was created in 1967, initially to address security concerns. In 1976 ASEAN developed a system of preferential trading arrangements and initiated various joint development projects. In January 1992, ASEAN heads of state agreed to establish the ASEAN Free Trade Area. A new, common effective preferential tariff scheme will be introduced, covering 38,680 items representing 88 percent of tariff lines. Tariffs will be reduced to 5 percent on some "fast-track" products by the year 2000 and on all covered products by 2007. AFTA will also provide for the removal of quantitative restrictions.

The formation of an East Asian Economic Group was suggested to address the potential threat of trade blocs elsewhere by promoting a common position and possible preferential trade agreements in East Asia. The proposed membership included ASEAN, China, Japan, and the NIEs. Most potential members did not endorse the earlier EAEG, and the concept was recast as the East Asian Economic Caucus, which is seen as promoting "open regionalism." There have also been several bilateral trade agreements among the East Asian economies and with trading partners outside the region, such as the China-Japan, U.S.-Singapore, and U.S.-Philippines trade agreements. Although current political and economic circumstances do not favor an East Asian bloc, stronger regional links and growing external discrimination could revive such a concept in the future.

The region's broadest institution is APEC, frequently likened to the OECD. APEC was launched in 1989 as an offshoot of two earlier quasi-governmental organizations, the Pacific Basin Economic Council founded in 1967 and the Pacific Economic Cooperation Council. A small APEC secretariat was established in Singapore in 1992. APEC's membership includes East Asia—including China, Hong Kong, and Taiwan (China)—North America, and Australasia. APEC has initiated working groups on trade and investment data, trade promotion, investment and technology transfer, human resources development, energy cooperation, marine resources, telecommunications, transportation, tourism, and fisheries. In 1993—for the first time—an APEC meeting was attended by the heads of most member states, and it is now likely that future meetings will also be conducted at this level. APEC's mission is still evolving. Because of its support for open regionalism, many see it as an important forum for the discussion of regional trade issues and as an effective counterweight to discriminatory initiatives.

In sum, East Asia's institutional structure is fluid. A healthy balance exists among institutions addressing different levels of international cooperation. Eventually these institutions could evolve into a hierarchy, offering problem-solving capacity at various regional levels. The region's economic leadership is also fluid: ASEAN, China, Korea, Japan, and Australia all play important roles in the region's economy. The region has ample policy infrastructure for undertaking ambitious regional initiatives, and this framework appears to be still open to new, forward-looking strategies.

Policy Options

The countries of the region will have to make decisions about the direction of their international economic policy. Two key considerations will dominate these decisions. The first is whether the policies adopted are open or discriminatory toward trade partners outside East Asia. The second is whether the group adopting these policies is small (with several countries in the region excluded) or large. These two considerations interact to create four policy options—not mutually exclusive—for trade liberalization: (1) a small group that is open, (2) a large group that is open, (3) a small group that is preferential, or (4) a large group that is preferential (table 5.1).

Option 1 involves MFN liberalization by one country or a small number of countries. This option comes closest to East Asia's traditional model of liberalization. Option 2 envisions broad agreement on MFN measures and actions that extend the benefits of regional liberalization to partners worldwide. Options 1 and 2 fall in the same spectrum of nondiscriminatory actions. Option 3 consists of relatively small preferential trade areas organized by one or more subregional trading groups. (By implication, these groups would discriminate against some significant players in the region.) Option 4 also entails an exclusive preferential scheme but with a broad membership that would discriminate against extraregional trade partners.

The arguments for Option 1—unilateral or small-group liberalization—rest on East Asia's success with this approach. Nearly all East Asian countries have unilaterally reduced protection over time because they believed outward-oriented policies could contribute to economic growth. If anything, these argu-

Nondiscriminatory liberalization is feasible—and economically preferable.

TABLE 5.1   POLICY OPTIONS IN THE EAST ASIA REGION

	Small group	*Large group*
Nondiscriminatory	**Option 1:** Unilateral or small-group MFN liberalization	**Option 2:** Regionwide MFN liberalization
Preferential	**Option 3:** Small trade bloc, such as a free trade area among a few countries	**Option 4:** Large trade bloc, such as a regionwide free trade area

ments have been reinforced by recent changes in East Asia's trading and investment environment. However, the incentives for this approach could be stronger if a country could also count on parallel liberalization by its trading partners.

Option 3—a small group with preferential agreements—may be the easiest to achieve. Smaller groups, such as ASEAN, may have more complementary objectives and be better able to control free-rider problems than larger groups. The markets encompassed by AFTA are small, especially if Singapore is not considered (it is already open). AFTA's economies also tend to be competitive rather than complementary; their intraregional trade accounted for 14 percent of total trade.

Option 4, a large preferential area for the East Asia region, would be less likely to divert trade because it would encompass an exceptionally diverse regional production system. But a preferential East Asian area could encourage inward-looking and possibly confrontational policies by other blocs and undermine the prospects of countries without access to regional blocs. A regionwide free trade agreement would be complex to negotiate, since it would have to cover a very wide range of economic systems. Since Article XXIV of the GATT requires that a preferential trade area eliminate all internal barriers, many sensitive issues would have to be tackled at once.

The advantages, but not the disadvantages, of a regionwide preferential bloc largely carry over to Option 2, a regionwide liberalization program implemented on an MFN basis. (This option really is on the same continuum as Option 1, except that all countries are envisaged to liberalize.) The high ratio of East Asia's intraregional trade to its total trade ensures that regional gains would be at least as large as under the preferential approach of Option 3 or 4. In addition, other countries would gain from East Asia's further opening to the rest of the world. The incentive to participate in a regionwide program might therefore be strong, since MFN liberalization would involve little risk of trade diversion. MFN liberalization could also focus initially on sectors in which regional complementarity is especially high or where resource endowments, transport costs, or technological differences limit outside competition. Elek (1992a and 1992b) identified processed minerals, textiles, and services as three sectors that meet these criteria. Because an MFN program would not have to comply with Article XXIV of the GATT, it could selectively lower some barriers. This would make balanced concession packages far easier to achieve. This option could complement any further efforts individual countries pursue under Option 1.

Benefits of the Trade and Investment Policy Options

The precise effects of the various policy options will depend on the specifics of trade and investment reforms agreed to by the regional partners, and in the absence of such specifics, a quantitative analysis of these policy options can only be indicative. Nevertheless, it is useful to develop at least a rough estimate of the benefits of a major East Asian liberalization.

A General Equilibrium Model

Martin and Yanagishima (1993) constructed a simple general equilibrium model to provide a preliminary assessment of these policy options. The model estimates a considerably more comprehensive set of gains from the liberalization than has been customary.

Six major types of effects of trade liberalization were considered:

- *Efficiency and welfare gains.* Liberalization replaces high-cost domestic goods with lower-cost foreign goods and permits consumption to expand. Both lower prices and greater consumption contribute to welfare gains. When trade liberalization is discriminatory, it can also lead to trade diversion from efficient outside exporters to inefficient inside exporters.
- *Terms-of-trade effects.* When countries produce goods differentiated from those of other countries, the trade gains from liberalization may reduce the price received for exports and increase the price paid for imports—and that price effect tends to decrease welfare in the liberalizing economy.
- *Firm-level economies of scale.* An increase in foreign competition due to liberalization reduces the markup and, in the medium term, increases the output of efficient domestic firms, which in turn reduces average cost—just as if technical progress had increased productivity.
- *Induced changes in foreign investment.* By improving access to foreign producers' goods (including raw materials, components, and capital goods), liberalization helps to attract investment from foreign multinationals that are pursuing global production strategies. Such investment, in turn, can increase the productivity of domestic factors of production.
- *Productivity gains from trade.* In addition to the initial increase in the level of output, greater openness has been observed to lead to higher growth in output. The potential explanations for this phenomenon include the availability of new and specialized inputs from world markets, the possibility of continuous innovation in products and processes to improve productivity, and greater research and development by firms when their potential market is larger.

■ *Positive feedback from concerted liberalization.* When several countries are liberalizing at the same time, the positive effects are reinforced.
In particular, terms-of-trade effects are more favorable than under unilateral liberalization, as each country's exports expand along with its
imports.

The effects of trade liberalization were estimated using the World Bank's
baseline projections of GDP, trade, and capital flows until the year 2000. The
baseline assumes that reforms of macroeconomic policies lead to an annual
global economic growth rate of roughly 3.2 percent (2.7 percent in the industrial countries and 5.2 percent in the developing countries) on average over the
next decade. East Asia is expected to grow at nearly 8 percent under this base
scenario of sound policies.

The data on trade protection include detailed matrices of tariff levels for
different countries obtained from the Bank's data base and updated for the recent changes under the Uruguay Round and NAFTA. These matrices were then
inflated to approximate total (tariff and nontariff) protection, using somewhat
judgmentally derived ratios of the size of quantitative restrictions to tariffs.

The liberalization package under consideration was assumed to reduce
protection levels to half the base levels. Foreign direct investment into liberalizing developing countries was assumed to double from the base case under the
broad-based MFN-type liberalization and to increase by 50 percent in the cases
of more limited liberalization. The rationale is that a broad-based liberalization
would enable companies to implement their globalization strategies more effectively and thus would induce larger FDI flows.

Option 2 results in relatively greater improvements in trade and output for
each country group (table 5.2). The reasons include the much stronger productivity gains from the MFN-type liberalization and the larger-scale effects from
the countries liberalizing in a concerted way. The trade and output effects under
Option 3 are generally positive, while the effects are mildly negative for its
trading partners in the region and elsewhere. East Asian countries benefit
slightly if the preferential bloc is extended to cover all of the region (Option 4),
but the effects on other trading partners are slightly negative. The benefits for
the individual liberalizing countries are at least as good as in policy Option 3 if
they liberalize unilaterally on an MFN basis (Option 1). There may be some
positive effects for the world economy from unilateral liberalization, but they
are small.

The estimates shown in table 5.2 for Option 1 indicate the gains for ASEAN
if it liberalizes alone. But if only one country or one group liberalizes, the others
would not enjoy many benefits. The impact on nonliberalizing countries would
be similar to that in Option 3, in which a small group liberalizes and the others

Gains would be greatest under Option 2.

TABLE 5.2   TRADE AND INCOME EFFECTS OF LIBERALIZATION OPTIONS
(percentage change in level)

Country group	Option 1: Unilateral MFN liberalization (ASEAN as an example)[a]			Option 2: East Asian MFN liberalization		
	Exports	Imports	Real income	Exports	Imports	Real income
China	0.01	0.01	0.02	14.6	20.9	3.9
ASEAN	3.70	5.40	4.20	4.1	8.2	5.0
NIES	0.30	0.05	0.04	6.0	4.6	1.4
Japan	0.90	0.40	0.08	3.1	2.0	0.2
European Union	0.03	−0.01	0.01	0.2	−0.1	0.1
United States	0.08	−0.15	0.00	0.6	−0.3	0.1
World	0.30	0.30	0.10	1.4	1.4	0.4[b]

Country group	Option 3: Small-group preferential liberalization (ASEAN as an example)			Option 4: East Asian preferential liberalization		
	Exports	Imports	Real income	Exports	Imports	Real income
China	−0.10	−0.10	0.00	10.5	13.1	1.8
ASEAN	2.90	4.50	2.10	3.7	5.5	3.0
NIES	0.00	−0.30	−0.10	4.8	4.3	1.0
Japan	0.10	−0.50	0.00	3.9	3.7	0.4
European Union	0.00	0.00	0.00	−0.1	−0.2	−0.1
United States	0.00	−0.20	0.00	−0.5	−0.8	−0.1
World	0.20	0.20	0.04	1.0	1.0	0.2

a. Data reflect action by ASEAN countries only. Similar results are obtained for the cases of unilateral MFN liberalization by China, Japan, and the NIEs.
b. This does not include income-generating effects in investor countries. Thus, the full positive impact on Japan, the European Union, or the United States, for instance, could be much larger.
Source: Martin and Yanagishima (1993); Martin, Petri, and Yanagishima (1994); World Bank staff estimates.

do not. There is no advantage for East Asian countries to free-ride on the liberalization of others. And there are significant benefits to regional action. Option 2 is a strong variant of Option 1, with all the countries taking MFN action.

The absolute benefits under Option 2 in income and trade would also be large—about one-half of the benefits of the Uruguay Round, itself one of the most ambitious programs of trade liberalization in recent history (table 5.3). The global increase in income under Option 2 is estimated to be more than $100

East Asian MFN liberalization could produce benefits equivalent to one-half of those resulting from the Uruguay Round agreements.

TABLE 5.3   EXPECTED TRADE AND INCOME BENEFITS OF EAST ASIAN LIBERALIZATION
UNDER OPTION 2

(billions of 1987 dollars)

Country group	Export value	Import value	Trade balance	Real income
China	25	39	−14	36
ASEAN	22	44	−22	34
NIES	41	31	10	22
Japan	21	11	10	7
European Union	5	−2	6	2
United States	7	−3	10	4
World	120	120	0	106

Source: Martin, Petri, and Yanagishima (1994); World Bank staff estimates.

billion over the level for the year 2000. The major beneficiaries would be in East Asia itself because of the concerted liberalization, the strong trade links in the region, and the efficiency gains and cost reductions generated by the actions. So even though the liberalization would be on an MFN basis, the bulk of the direct benefits would be in the region. Under the package, low- and middle-income East Asia would incur an additional trade deficit of about $36 billion, but that would be balanced by increased investment flows.

An outcome of Option 2 is that there would be small gains for the region's major industrial country trading partners. That these welfare gains would be less than those enjoyed by the liberalizing countries/region is to be expected. Liberalizing countries benefit the most from liberalization, but partners also benefit from income and trade balance improvements. This is very significant for the economic and political sustainability of East Asia's export-oriented growth strategy toward the rest of the world. By taking a leading role in liberalizing trade and reducing barriers to exports from the United States and Europe, East Asian countries will be able to defuse some of the tension caused by their large trade surpluses and discourage other countries from introducing countervailing measures by offering greater trading opportunities. The trade deficits of the industrial countries outside East Asia tend to decline as the region liberalizes trade and attracts FDI. The precise nature of the balance-of-payments outcome, of course, depends also on the macroeconomic policies outside the region.

The model underestimates the positive impact on Pacific and European exports. By concerted liberalization beyond the Uruguay Round, including reducing quantitative restrictions, the East Asian countries can send an unmistakable signal about their intentions to welcome stronger trading relations. This will help dispel impressions that their markets are hard to penetrate and will encourage new and renewed export efforts by producers in the industrial countries. Furthermore, the model indicates that liberalized investment policies that attract more FDI from North America and Europe will also lead to higher exports from these countries into East Asia. The income-generating effects of FDI in the source countries are not fully captured by the model.

A Model of Global Economic Growth

In a different analysis using the World Bank's Global Economic Model, a baseline forecast of global outcomes was carried out (World Bank 1994b; Armington 1994). The salient assumptions included (a) continued low interest rates, low inflation, and substantial private capital flows, keeping the economic recovery going in the OECD countries; (b) gains from the completion of the Uruguay Round and NAFTA; and (c) the stabilization of commodity prices. The resulting base case numbers for output and trade were employed in the previous model as well: the projected average growth rate over the next decade is over 8 percent for China, 6 to 7 percent for ASEAN and the NIEs, and 2 to 3 percent for Japan and other OECD countries.

The analysis was extended to consider a scenario in which East Asia leads the next phase of trade liberalization under the GATT rules, reducing tariffs by an additional 50 percent. FDI flows to developing East Asia would then more than double from the baseline, with the additional resources coming from Europe, Japan, the NIEs, and the United States.

This package is estimated to add about 1.6 percent to world trade and over 0.4 percent to world output from the baseline. Not surprisingly, East Asia would be the main beneficiary of the initiative: ASEAN, China, and the NIEs would gain about 3 percent in real GDP over the baseline. There would also be small but pervasive spillovers to other regions: the OECD countries, including Japan, would gain 0.1 to 0.2 percent, with gains of about twice that much for developing regions outside East Asia. These effects would continue over time.

Under this scenario, developing East Asia would have a current account deficit of about $58 billion—higher than the baseline estimate, but financed by higher FDI flows from the NIEs and OECD countries. Japan's surplus would be only $7 billion—lower than the baseline estimate.

In one scenario of downside risks, higher barriers around the European Union and NAFTA countries result from failures to control unemployment, fiscal deficits, and trade deficits. These barriers lead to a reduction of world trade by

1.5 percent a year and a loss in GDP growth relative to the baseline of 0.8 percent a year.

East Asian leadership in the liberalization of trade and investment is likely to reduce protectionist policy pressures in other parts of the world and thereby improve the odds for international economic cooperation. Thus, the potential benefits of the approach are the gains inherent in that approach plus the expected gains from preventing the low-case scenario. The estimated 0.8 percent decline in the growth rate under the downside scenario suggests that even a small reduction in the probability of such impairment in growth would be important; it would translate into substantial gains for East Asia and the rest of the world.

Conclusion: A Win-Win Approach

The study has concentrated on the evolution of trade, its contribution to growth, and the positive impact of FDI on growth and export expansion in East Asia. The objective was to determine whether the successful trade-driven strategies of the region can remain economically and politically viable and can strengthen relations with the region's key trading partners. The analysis confirms that outward orientation has been and will continue to be a major factor in the rapid growth of East Asian economies. It also shows that there is further scope for increasing intraregional trade and that the benefits from further trade liberalization would be enhanced by greater openness to FDI.

Several options (not mutually exclusive) for further liberalization were considered. Unilateral reform and preferential blocs were found to benefit the country or group of countries engaging in liberalization, but they offered small benefits or possible losses to trading partners, thus not satisfying the second part of the sustainability criterion. Concerted MFN trade liberalization by East Asian economies was found to offer greater welfare benefits to the region as well as real welfare gains (and trade deficit reduction) to major trading partners outside the region. The analysis concentrated on the benefits to the region because that is where the key decisions to change policy need to be justified and made.

It is also crucial that the rest of the world take no negative actions to inhibit trade relations with these countries. Such actions would have adverse welfare effects for both parties. A positive response through MFN trade liberalization by others would reinforce the proposed approach and benefit all parties. Such support should enhance the sustainability of the proposed reforms.

In sum, concerted multilateral trade and investment liberalization benefits the economies of the region and the global economy. The approach is consistent with the GATT because it follows the nondiscriminatory MFN approach. It also suggests modes of cooperation that could serve as a model for future worldwide efforts. The approach does not call for detailed negotiations of exact policy changes across countries, but rather a common MFN approach in the region.

This analysis leads to a proposal with six major elements:

- In East Asian countries, a reduction in tariffs and the tariff equivalent of quantitative restrictions by, say, 50 percent from the base levels agreed to in the Uruguay Round.
- A program to liberalize FDI policies in developing East Asia and mobilize FDI from other parts of the region and the world, leading to a doubling of FDI flows from baseline projections.
- Cooperation on issues that affect trade and economic integration, especially environmental protection and other areas such as safety standards and the development of infrastructure.
- Commitment by OECD countries to follow nondiscriminatory MFN approaches in trade and investment and to eschew unilateralism.
- Assistance from multilateral agencies in designing and implementing reform programs for developing East Asia and in augmenting FDI flows to the region.
- Technical advice and financing from OECD countries and multilateral agencies to deal with the environmental and infrastructure implications of East Asia's integration initiatives.

The proposed East Asian liberalization approach is a win-win solution for world trade tensions. By assuming a leading role in multilateral, nonpreferential liberalization, East Asia could further strengthen the GATT process—while at the same time, the OECD countries could refrain from inward-looking approaches and promote further multilateralism. Furthermore, the integration of trade and investment liberalization programs, supported by investment from capital-surplus countries, would bring developing countries further into the mainstream of global trade reform. The initiative would thus reinvigorate the principles of multilateralism that have served the world economy—and the East Asia region—so well in the post–World War II period.

Notes

1. In this report, "East Asia" comprises the low- and middle-income countries of the region—China, Indonesia, Malaysia, the Philippines, and Thailand—along with Japan and the newly industrializing economies—Hong Kong, the Republic of Korea, Singapore, and Taiwan (China). "Developing East Asia" means East Asia excluding Japan. The "Pacific region" comprises Australia, East Asia, New Zealand, and North America.

2. ASEAN comprises Brunei, Indonesia, Malaysia, the Philippines, Singapore, and Thailand.

3. Regional biases within East Asian trade (measured by the gravity coefficients) remained at essentially the same high level in 1955 as in 1938.

4. For example, if Thailand's exports to Singapore account for 3 percent of Singapore's Pacific Rim imports, and if Thailand's exports account for 1 percent of total Pacific Rim imports, the gravity coefficient of Thailand's exports to Singapore is 3; the linkage is three times as intense as expected under a proportional distribution of intra-Pacific trade.

5. Progress—in varying degrees—is being made across the East Asian countries, but comparable data on the more recent changes are not available. The estimates of protection given here therefore do not include the reforms of recent months.

6. The estimates for China are somewhat imprecise. There is, for instance, the problem of "round tripping" FDI, brought about by the tax concessions for joint ventures.

Appendix Tables

Table A-1   Basic Indicators, 1992

Economy	Population (millions)	GDP growth (percent)	Inflation rate (percent)	Ratio of current account balance to GDP (percent)
East Asia				
China	1,162.2	12.8	6.8	1.5
Hong Kong	5.8	5.0	9.6	—
Indonesia	184.3	6.3	7.5	−2.9
Japan	124.5	1.3	1.7	3.2
Korea, Rep. of	43.7	4.8	6.2	−1.5
Malaysia	18.6	8.0	4.8	−3.0
Philippines	64.3	0.0	8.9	−1.9
Singapore	2.8	5.8	2.3	6.4
Thailand	58.0	7.5	4.1	−6.1
Viet Nam	69.4	8.3	—	—
Other Pacific region countries				
Australia	17.5	1.8	1.0	−3.6
Canada	27.4	0.7	1.5	−4.1
Mexico	85.0	1.9	15.5	−6.9
New Zealand	3.4	2.8	1.0	−1.9
United States	255.4	2.6	3.0	−1.1

—   Not available.

Source: World Bank data.

Table A-2   Selected Economic Indicators, 1992

	Annual growth rate (percent)		Share of GDP (percent)		
Economy	Exports	Imports	Gross domestic investment	Gross domestic savings	Resource balance
East Asia					
China	15.5	29.1	34.1	35.1	1.0
Hong Kong	18.1	20.7	28.8	30.5	1.7
Indonesia	16.4	7.1	35.0	37.0	3.0
Japan	4.9	0.0	31.0	34.0	2.0
Korea, Rep. of	9.8	2.9	36.4	—	—
Malaysia	8.4	1.6	34.0	35.0	1.0
Philippines	1.2	13.2	22.6	18.0	−4.7
Singapore	5.7	6.1	40.8	46.9	6.2
Taiwan (China)	6.5	12.2	23.9	26.7	2.7
Thailand	10.7	7.1	40.0	35.0	−5.0
Other Pacific region countries					
Australia	5.3	6.8	20.4	19.4	−1.0
Canada	7.9	4.9	19.0	18.0	−1.0
Mexico	0.2	21.2	24.0	17.0	−7.0
New Zealand	0.3	8.0	19.0	20.0	1.0
United States	6.3	8.7	16.0	15.0	−1.0

— Not available.

Source: World Bank data.

Table A-3   Average Annual Growth of Production, 1980–92
(percent)

Economy	GDP	Agriculture	Industry	Manufac- turing	Services
East Asia	7.7	4.4	9.4	10.6[a]	8.9
China	9.1	5.4	11.1	11.1[a]	11.0
Hong Kong	6.7	—	—	—	—
Indonesia	5.7	3.1	6.1	12.0	6.8
Japan	4.1	0.7[a]	5.1[a]	5.8[a]	3.7[a]
Korea, Rep. of	9.4	1.9	11.6	11.9	9.3
Malaysia	5.9	3.6	8.0	10.0	5.1
Philippines	1.2	1.0	−0.2	0.7	2.8
Singapore	6.7	−6.6[a]	6.0[a]	7.1	7.3
Thailand	8.2	4.1	10.1	10.1	8.1
Other Pacific region countries					
Australia	3.1	2.9[a]	2.2[a]	1.4[a]	4.0[a]
Canada	2.8	1.6[a]	2.4[a]	2.4[a]	3.1[a]
Mexico	1.5	0.6	1.6	2.1	1.5
New Zealand	1.4	3.8[a]	1.3[a]	0.7[a]	1.7[a]
United States	2.7	—	—	—	2.9
Other regions					
Europe and Central Asia	1.5[a]	—	—	—	—
Latin America and the Caribbean	1.8	2.0	1.3	0.8	2.1
Middle East and North Africa	2.2	4.7	0.9	4.5	1.4
South Asia	5.2	3.3	6.4	6.5	6.2
Sub-Saharan Africa	1.8	1.7	1.2	1.4	2.3

— Not available.

a. Growth rates are for years other than 1980–92.

Source: World Bank (1994c).

Table A-4 Distribution of East Asian Trade, 1988–92

(percentage shares)

Trading partner	Exports					Imports				
	1988	1989	1990	1991	1992	1988	1989	1990	1991	1992
East Asia	35.6	36.8	38.0	40.0	40.5	42.6	42.2	41.9	45.0	47.0
China	4.9	4.8	4.2	5.1	6.6	5.1	4.9	4.8	5.0	5.2
Hong Kong	6.0	5.7	6.0	6.3	6.6	3.9	3.6	3.6	4.0	4.4
Indonesia	0.9	1.0	1.3	1.3	1.3	2.5	2.6	2.7	2.7	2.8
Japan	8.7	9.0	8.8	8.5	7.9	15.5	15.2	14.7	15.8	16.3
Korea, Rep. of	3.6	3.6	3.7	4.1	3.3	3.8	3.8	3.5	3.8	4.0
Malaysia	1.8	2.1	2.3	2.8	2.4	3.1	3.0	3.1	3.4	3.4
Philippines	0.8	0.9	0.9	0.9	1.0	0.7	0.6	0.6	0.6	0.6
Singapore	3.7	3.9	4.4	4.6	4.7	2.4	2.7	2.9	3.1	3.2
Taiwan (China)	3.4	3.5	3.6	3.8	4.0	4.1	4.2	4.4	4.8	5.0
Thailand	1.8	2.1	2.7	2.5	2.4	1.3	1.5	1.5	1.6	1.8
Viet Nam	0.1	0.1	0.1	0.2	0.3	0.1	0.1	0.2	0.2	0.2

Other Pacific region countries	34.7	34.8	31.7	29.6	29.6	26.3	26.4	25.3	24.7	23.6
Australia	2.1	2.3	2.0	1.8	1.8	3.5	3.7	3.6	3.6	3.5
Canada	2.1	2.1	1.9	1.9	1.8	2.7	2.4	2.2	2.0	1.9
Mexico	0.4	0.5	0.6	0.6	0.8	0.5	0.4	0.4	0.4	0.3
New Zealand	0.3	0.4	0.3	0.3	0.3	0.6	0.6	0.5	0.5	0.5
United States	29.8	29.5	27.0	25.0	24.9	19.0	19.2	18.6	18.2	17.4
European Union[a]	15.8	15.5	16.7	17.0	16.4	13.0	13.1	14.1	13.1	13.1
Rest of the world	13.8	12.9	13.5	13.4	13.5	18.2	18.3	18.7	17.1	16.4
Total	100.0	100.0	100.0	100.0	100.0	100.0	100.0	100.0	100.0	100.0
Total (billions of dollars)	591	633	687	768	839	449	503	571	642	703

Note: Both exports and imports are in free-on-board prices. Data may not add to totals because of rounding. Data for China and Hong Kong have been adjusted to remove the effects of reexports.

a. Comprising only the original twelve members of the European Community.

Source: IMF *Direction of Trade Statistics* (various issues); World Bank staff estimates.

Table A-5 Distribution of Australian, New Zealand, and North American Trade, 1988–92
(percentage shares)

Trading partner	Exports					Imports				
	1988	1989	1990	1991	1992	1988	1989	1990	1991	1992
East Asia	23.8	24.1	23.9	24.1	23.4	33.1	32.3	30.5	32.0	32.6
China	1.7	1.4	1.2	1.5	1.6	1.7	2.2	2.6	3.2	3.9
Hong Kong	1.7	1.6	1.4	1.7	1.7	2.0	1.7	1.6	1.6	1.6
Indonesia	0.4	0.4	0.6	0.5	0.7	0.6	0.6	0.6	0.6	0.8
Japan	11.3	11.7	11.6	10.8	10.0	17.1	16.5	15.1	15.6	15.2
Korea, Rep. of	2.8	3.1	3.1	3.2	2.7	3.8	3.4	3.1	2.9	2.6
Malaysia	0.6	0.7	0.8	0.8	0.8	0.7	0.8	0.9	1.0	1.2
Philippines	0.5	0.5	0.5	0.4	0.5	0.5	0.5	0.5	0.5	0.6
Singapore	1.4	1.6	1.7	1.8	1.9	1.5	1.5	1.6	1.6	1.7
Taiwan (China)	2.8	2.5	2.3	2.6	2.7	4.6	4.2	3.7	3.8	3.8
Thailand	0.5	0.6	0.7	0.7	0.8	0.6	0.8	0.9	1.0	1.0
Viet Nam	0.0	0.0	0.0	0.0	0.0	0.0	0.0	0.0	0.0	0.0

Other Pacific region countries	40.9	40.8	41.5	41.6	43.1	33.9	35.1	35.5	36.4	36.6
Australia	1.9	2.0	1.9	1.7	1.7	0.9	0.9	1.0	0.9	0.8
Canada	14.2	14.3	14.1	13.8	13.8	12.8	12.9	12.8	12.8	12.8
Mexico	4.2	4.6	4.9	5.3	6.1	3.8	4.1	4.4	4.6	4.8
New Zealand	0.5	0.6	0.5	0.5	0.5	0.5	0.5	0.5	0.5	0.4
United States	20.1	19.3	20.1	20.4	20.9	15.9	16.7	16.9	17.6	17.8
European Union[a]	18.8	19.1	19.9	19.2	18.1	18.0	16.6	17.3	16.1	15.9
Rest of the world	16.5	16.1	14.7	15.1	15.4	14.9	16.0	16.7	15.5	14.9
Total	100.0	100.0	100.0	100.0	100.0	100.0	100.0	100.0	100.0	100.0
Total (billions of dollars)	498	553	595	639	675	607	659	710	715	775

Note: Both exports and imports are in free-on-board prices. Data may not add to totals because of rounding. Data for China and Hong Kong have been adjusted to remove the effects of reexports.

a. Comprising only the original twelve members of the European Community.

Source: IMF *Direction of Trade Statistics* (various issues).

Table A-6　Distribution of the European Union's Trade, 1988–92
(percentage shares)

Trading partner	Exports					Imports				
	1988	1989	1990	1991	1992	1988	1989	1990	1991	1992
East Asia	5.3	5.6	5.7	5.8	5.9	9.3	9.1	8.9	9.8	9.9
China	0.6	0.6	0.5	0.5	0.6	0.7	0.8	0.9	1.2	1.3
Hong Kong	0.6	0.6	0.6	0.7	0.7	0.8	0.7	0.7	0.7	0.7
Indonesia	0.2	0.2	0.3	0.3	0.4	0.2	0.2	0.3	0.3	0.4
Japan	1.9	2.0	2.1	2.0	1.8	4.6	4.5	4.3	4.5	4.5
Korea, Rep. of	0.5	0.5	0.6	0.6	0.6	0.8	0.7	0.6	0.7	0.6
Malaysia	0.2	0.2	0.2	0.3	0.3	0.3	0.4	0.4	0.4	0.5
Philippines	0.1	0.1	0.1	0.1	0.1	0.1	0.1	0.1	0.1	0.1
Singapore	0.4	0.5	0.5	0.5	0.5	0.4	0.4	0.5	0.5	0.5
Taiwan (China)	0.5	0.5	0.4	0.5	0.5	0.9	0.9	0.8	1.0	0.9
Thailand	0.2	0.3	0.3	0.3	0.3	0.3	0.3	0.4	0.4	0.4
Viet Nam	0.0	0.0	0.0	0.0	0.0	0.0	0.0	0.0	0.0	0.0

Other Pacific region countries	10.1	9.8	9.0	8.3	8.4	9.2	9.7	9.1	9.3	8.8
Australia	0.7	0.8	0.6	0.6	0.6	0.5	0.5	0.4	0.4	0.4
New Zealand	0.1	0.1	0.1	0.1	0.1	0.2	0.2	0.1	0.1	0.1
North America	9.3	8.9	8.3	7.7	7.8	8.5	9.0	8.6	8.8	8.3
European Union	59.5	59.7	60.6	61.8	61.4	57.7	57.2	57.8	57.6	58.2
Rest of the world	25.2	24.9	24.7	24.1	24.3	23.8	24.1	24.2	23.3	23.0
Total	100.0	100.0	100.0	100.0	100.0	100.0	100.0	100.0	100.0	100.0
Total (billions of dollars)	1,065	1,136	1,366	1,371	1,456	1,044	1,125	1,355	1,401	1,465

Note: The European Union comprises only the original twelve members of the European Community. Both exports and imports are in free-on-board prices. Data may not add to totals because of rounding. Data for China and Hong Kong have been adjusted to remove the effects of reexports.

Source: IMF *Direction of Trade Statistics* (various issues).

Table A-7 Commodity Composition of East Asian Exports
(percentage shares)

Economy	Food and live animals		Beverages and tobacco		Crude materials excluding fuels		Mineral fuels, etc.		Animal and vegetable oils and fats	
	1980	1991	1980	1991	1980	1991	1980	1991	1980	1991
East Asia	45	58	28	74	60	67	67	79	25	38
China	1	1	3	3	4	5	0	3	2	11
Hong Kong	4	10	4	20	2	8	4	5	1	3
Indonesia	5	1	1	0	1	2	0	1	0	1
Japan	20	32	9	22	29	28	45	38	4	5
Korea, Rep. of	3	4	0	5	6	8	1	8	1	3
Malaysia	4	3	4	4	1	2	3	4	0	1
Philippines	1	1	0	1	0	1	2	1	0	0
Singapore	5	5	2	7	10	4	8	7	13	10
Taiwan (China)	2	2	3	10	6	6	1	4	0	2
Thailand	1	2	1	1	1	2	3	6	2	0
Viet Nam	0	0	1	0	0	0	0	0	0	0

Other Pacific region countries	16	15	12	5	10	10	23	8	14	10
Australia	1	1	1	1	1	1	3	2	1	1
Canada	1	1	0	0	1	1	0	0	1	1
Mexico	0	0	0	0	0	0	0	0	0	1
New Zealand	0	0	0	0	0	0	2	0	0	0
United States	13	12	11	4	7	7	18	6	12	7
European Union[a]	19	13	26	9	17	14	1	2	25	21
Rest of the world	20	14	33	11	13	10	9	10	36	32
Total (billions of dollars)	11	29	1	3	15	18	25	35	3	4

(Table continues on the following page.)

Table A-7 Commodity Composition of East Asian Exports (*continued*)

(percentage shares)

Economy	Chemicals and related products		Basic manufactures		Machines and transport equipment		Other manufactured goods		Other	
	1980	1991	1980	1991	1980	1991	1980	1991	1980	1991
East Asia	54	61	35	56	22	32	15	33	28	33
China	6	7	5	5	2	2	1	2	2	3
Hong Kong	4	13	6	17	3	7	4	14	4	6
Indonesia	5	3	3	2	2	1	0	0	1	1
Japan	5	6	4	9	1	3	5	9	6	3
Korea, Rep. of	9	9	3	5	2	4	1	2	4	3
Malaysia	5	5	2	3	3	3	1	1	3	3
Philippines	3	2	2	1	1	1	0	0	1	1
Singapore	3	4	4	5	3	5	2	2	4	7
Taiwan (China)	7	8	4	5	3	4	1	2	2	4
Thailand	4	4	2	4	1	3	0	1	1	2
Viet Nam	0	1	0	0	0	0	0	0	0	0

Other Pacific region countries	15	15	23	19	36	35	40	36	27	33
Australia	3	2	2	2	3	2	2	1	2	2
Canada	1	1	2	1	2	2	3	2	1	1
Mexico	1	0	1	1	1	1	0	0	0	0
New Zealand	1	0	1	0	0	0	0	0	0	0
United States	10	12	18	15	30	30	35	31	24	30
European Union[a]	10	14	11	10	15	19	27	21	21	13
Rest of the world	22	10	32	15	27	13	18	10	24	21
Total (billions of dollars)	9	34	49	108	94	357	35	126	4	9

Note: Commodity classification follows SITC 1-digit codes. Data may not add to totals because of rounding.

a. Comprising only the original twelve members of the European Community.

Source: United Nations commodity trade data base.

Table A-8 Commodity Composition of East Asian Imports

(percentage shares)

Economy	Food and live animals		Beverages and tobacco		Crude materials excluding fuels		Mineral fuels, etc.		Animal and vegetable oils and fats	
	1980	1991	1980	1991	1980	1991	1980	1991	1980	1991
East Asia	32	37	9	13	32	29	22	32	66	65
China	8	10	4	5	2	5	3	4	3	3
Hong Kong	1	1	1	2	1	1	0	0	1	1
Indonesia	2	2	0	0	8	3	11	12	1	5
Japan	2	2	0	2	2	3	0	1	4	2
Korea, Rep. of	3	3	0	0	1	1	0	1	1	0
Malaysia	1	2	1	1	10	8	2	5	51	43
Philippines	4	2	0	0	4	1	0	0	3	2
Singapore	1	1	1	2	0	1	4	7	3	7
Taiwan (China)	5	6	1	0	1	2	0	0	0	1
Thailand	5	6	1	0	2	2	0	0	0	1
Viet Nam	0	1	0	0	0	1	0	1	0	0

Other Pacific region countries	49	41	45	38	49	49	6	14	25	12
Australia	11	8	0	0	11	12	3	7	2	3
Canada	4	4	1	0	8	8	1	2	4	1
Mexico	0	0	0	0	1	1	0	1	0	0
New Zealand	2	3	0	0	1	2	0	0	1	1
United States	32	26	43	37	29	26	3	4	19	7
European Union[a]	5	7	40	43	1	5	0	0	3	10
Rest of the world	14	15	6	6	17	18	72	53	6	14
Total (billions of dollars)	24	54	2	8	35	57	99	97	1	2

(Table continues on the following page.)

Table A-8 Commodity Composition of East Asian Imports *(continued)*
(percentage shares)

Economy	Chemicals and related products		Basic manufactures		Machines and transport equipment		Other manufactured goods		Other	
	1980	1991	1980	1991	1980	1991	1980	1991	1980	1991
East Asia	29	34	55	55	43	55	51	66	22	20
China	3	4	7	10	1	4	10	30	1	2
Hong Kong	1	2	1	6	1	5	4	6	4	3
Indonesia	0	1	1	3	0	0	0	1	0	0
Japan	18	15	28	17	33	29	18	12	7	4
Korea, Rep. of	2	3	7	7	2	3	7	6	2	2
Malaysia	0	1	2	1	1	3	1	2	1	2
Philippines	0	0	1	0	0	0	1	0	1	1
Singapore	2	3	1	1	2	4	2	2	5	4
Taiwan (China)	2	4	5	9	3	5	7	6	1	2
Thailand	0	1	1	1	0	2	1	2	0	0
Viet Nam	0	0	0	0	0	0	0	0	0	0

Other Pacific region countries	36	30	18	15	32	23	21	15	31	41
Australia	1	1	3	3	1	1	1	0	1	10
Canada	2	2	2	2	1	1	0	0	1	3
Mexico	0	1	1	0	0	0	0	0	0	0
New Zealand	0	0	1	1	0	0	0	0	0	0
United States	32	26	11	9	30	22	20	14	28	27
European Union[a]	26	24	11	11	20	17	19	14	21	16
Rest of the world	8	12	16	19	5	4	9	6	26	24
Total (billions of dollars)	17	66	31	123	43	224	13	79	4	18

Note: Commodity classification follows SITC 1-digit codes. Data may not add to totals because of rounding.

a. Comprising only the original twelve members of the European Community.

Source: United Nations commodity trade data base.

Selected Bibliography

Akamatsu, K. 1960. "A Theory of Unbalanced Growth in the World Economy." *Weltwirtschaftliches Archiv* (Germany) 86(2).

Armington, Paul. 1994. "Simulations of East Asian Policy Packages Using Bank-GEM." Background paper for *East Asia's Trade and Investment*. World Bank, International Economics Department, Washington, D.C.

Baneth, Jean. 1993. *"Fortress Europe" and Other Myths about Trade: Policies toward Merchandise Imports in the EC and Other Major Industrial Economies (and What They Mean for Developing Countries)*. Discussion Paper 225. Washington, D.C.: World Bank.

Bannister, Geoffrey, and Carlos Braga. Forthcoming. "Intra-Asian Investment and Trade: Prospects for Growing Regionalization in the 1990s." Background paper for *East Asia's Trade and Investment*. World Bank, International Economics Department, Washington, D.C.

Bergsten, Fred C. 1991. "Commentary: The Move toward Free Trade Zones." *Economic Review/Federal Reserve Bank of Kansas City* 76(Nov.–Dec.): 27–35.

———. 1993. "Reconcilable Differences? United States–Japan Economic Conflict." Institute for International Economics, Washington, D.C.

Bhagwati, Jagdish. 1991. *The World Trading System at Risk*. Hemel Hempstead, U.K.: Harvester Wheatsheaf.

———. 1992. "Regionalism versus Multilateralism." *World Economy* (U.K.) 15(Sept.):535–55.

Bhattacharya, Amar, and Johannes F. Linn. 1988. *Trade and Industrial Policies in the Developing Countries of East Asia*. Discussion Paper 27. Washington, D.C: World Bank.

Braga, Carlos A., Raed Safadi, and Alexander Yeats. 1994. "Implications of NAFTA for East Asian Exports." Policy Research Working Paper. World Bank, International Economics Department, Washington, D.C.

Brandão, Antonio Salazar P., and Will Martin. 1992. "Implications of Agricultural Trade Liberalization for the Developing Countries." Policy Research Working Paper 1116. World Bank, International Economics Department, Washington, D.C.

Cline, William. 1985. "Imports of Manufactures from Developing Countries: Performance and Prospects for Market Access." Brookings Institution, Washington, D.C.

Cooper, Richard, and International Economic Association. 1974. *Worldwide versus Regional Integration: Is There an Optimal Size of the Integrated Area?* Discussion Paper 220. New Haven, Conn.: Yale University, Economic Growth Center.

Corden, W. Max. 1987a. *Protection and Liberalization: A Review of Analytical Issues.* IMF Occasional Paper. Washington, D.C.: International Monetary Fund.

————. 1987b. *Trade Policy and Economic Welfare.* Oxford, U.K.: Clarendon Press.

de Melo, Jaime, and Arvind Panagariya. 1992. "The New Regionalism." *Finance and Development* 29(Dec.): 37–40.

Dornbusch, Rudiger. 1992. "The Case for Trade Liberalization in Developing Countries." *Journal of Economic Perspectives* 6(Winter):69–85.

Drysdale, Peter. 1991. "Open Regionalism: A Key to East Asia's Economic Future." Pacific Economic Paper 197. Australia-Japan Research Center, Australian National University, Canberra.

Elek, Andrew. 1992a. "Pacific Economic Co-operation: Policy Choices for the 1990s." *Asian Pacific Economic Literature* (Australia) 6(May):1–15.

————. 1992b. "Trade Policy Options for the Asia-Pacific Region in the 1990's: The Potential of Open Regionalism." *American Economic Review, Papers and Proceedings* 82(May):74–78.

European Community. 1993. *International Economic Independence.* Discussion Paper. Brussels.

Finger, J. M. 1993. "GATT's Influence on Regional Arrangements." In Jaime de Melo and Arvind Panagariya, eds., *New Dimensions in Regional Integration.* Cambridge, U.K., and New York: Cambridge University Press.

Finger, J. Michael, and Rajat Kathuria. 1993. "Trade Liberalization: A Public Policy Perspective." Background paper for *East Asia's Trade and Investment.* World Bank, International Economics Department, Trade Policy Division, Washington, D.C.

Finger, J. Michael, and Andrzej Olechowski, eds. 1987. *The Uruguay Round: A Handbook for the Multilateral Trade Negotiations.* Washington, D.C.: World Bank.

Frankel, Jeffrey A. 1992. *Is Japan Creating a Yen Bloc in East Asia and the Pacific?* Working Paper 4050. Cambridge, Mass.: National Bureau of Economic Research.

Fukasaku, Kiichiro. 1992. "Economic Regionalization and Intra-Industry Trade: Pacific Asian Perspectives." Technical Paper 53. Development Center, Organization of Economic Cooperation and Development, Paris.

General Agreement on Tariffs and Trade. Various issues. *Trade Policy Review.* Geneva.

Government of Australia, East Asia Analytical Unit, Department of Foreign Affairs and Trade. 1994. *AFTA: Trading Bloc or Building Block?* Canberra: Australian Government Publishing Service.

Hill, Hal, and Brian Jones. 1985. "The Role of Direct Foreign Investment in Developing East Asian Countries." Australian Working Paper 18. Association of Southeast Asian Nations, Singapore.

Hong, Wontack, and Lawrence B. Krause, eds. 1981. *Trade and Growth of the Advanced Developing Countries in the Pacific Basin: Papers and Proceedings of the Eleventh Pacific Trade and Development Conference.* Seoul: Korea Development Institute.

Hudec, Robert E. 1990. "Section 301: Beyond Good and Evil." In J. Bhagwati and H. Patrick, eds., *Aggressive Unilateralism: America's 301 Trade Policy and the World Trading System*. Ann Arbor: University of Michigan Press.

IMF (International Monetary Fund). 1993. *Balance of Payments Statistics Yearbook*. Washington, D.C.

————. Various issues. *Direction of Trade Statistics*. Washington, D.C.

Irwin, Douglas. 1992. "Multilateral and Bilateral Trade Policies in the World Trading System: An Historical Perspective." Paper presented at the World Bank–CEPR Conference on New Dimensions in Regional Integration, April 2–3, World Bank, Washington, D.C.

Japan Institute for Overseas Investment. 1993. *Foreign Direct Investment in the East Asia Region: Trends and Outlook*. Tokyo.

Katseli, Louka T. 1992. "Foreign Direct Investment and Trade Linkages in the 1990's: Experience and Prospects of Developing Countries." Paper 687. Center for Economic Policy Research, London.

Kawaguchi, Osamu. 1994. "Foreign Direct Investment in East Asia: Trends, Determinants and Policy Implications." Internal discussion paper 139. World Bank, East Asia and the Pacific Region, Washington, D.C.

Kojima, Kiyoshi. 1985. "The Allocation of Japanese Direct Foreign Investment and Its Evolution in Asia." *Hitotsubashi Journal of Economics* 26(Dec.): 99–116.

Krugman, Paul. 1991. "Regionalism and Multilateralism: Analytical Notes." Paper presented at the World Bank–CEPR Conference on New Dimensions in Regional Integration, April 2–3, World Bank, Washington, D.C.

Lawrence, Robert Z. 1991. "Emerging Regional Arrangements: Building Blocks or Stumbling Blocks." *AMEX Bank Review* (U.K.) 18(Nov.): 4–5.

Leipziger, Danny M., and Vinod Thomas. 1993. *The Lessons of East Asia: An Overview of Country Experience*. Washington, D.C.: World Bank.

Lim, Linda Y. C., and Pang Eng Fong. 1991. *Foreign Direct Investment and Industrialization in Malaysia, Singapore, Taiwan and Thailand*. Paris: Development Center of the Organization for Economic Cooperation and Development.

Martin, Will, and Koji Yanagishima. 1993. "Concerted Trade Liberalization and Economic Development in the Asia-Pacific Region." Background paper for *East Asia's Trade and Investment*. World Bank, International Economics Department, Washington, D.C.

Martin, Will, Peter Petri, and Koji Yanagishima. 1994. "Charting the Pacific: An Empirical Assessment of Integration Initiatives." Background paper for *East Asia's Trade and Investment*. World Bank, International Economics Department, Washington, D.C.

Michaely, Michael, Armeane M. Choksi, and Demetris Papageorgiou. 1991. *Liberalizing Foreign Trade: Lessons of Experience in the Developing World*. Cambridge, U.K.: Basil Blackwell.

MITI (Ministry of International Trade and Investment), Government of Japan. Various issues. *Survey of Overseas Activities of Japanese Companies*. Tokyo.

Mody, Ashoka. Forthcoming. "Japanese Investment in Asia: A Micro Analysis of Determinants and Benefits." Background paper for *East Asia's Trade and Investment*. World Bank, Washington, D.C.

Murakami, Yasusuka, and Yutaka Kosai. 1986. *Japan in the Global Community: Its Role and Contribution on the Eve of the Twenty-First Century*. Tokyo: University of Tokyo Press.

OECD Trade Committee. 1992a. "Integration of Developing Countries into the International Trading System: Suggested Areas for Future Work." Paris.

———. 1992b. "Sustaining the Liberalization Process in Developing Countries: Project Overview and Suggested Areas for Future Work." Paris.

Panagariya, Arvind. 1993. "Should East Asia Go Regional? No and Yes." Background paper for *East Asia's Trade and Investment*. World Bank, International Economics Department, Trade Policy Division, Washington, D.C.

Patrick, Hugh. 1987. "The Management of the United States–Japan Trade Relationship and Its Implications for Pacific Basin Economies." Mimeo. U.S. National Committee for Pacific Economic Cooperation, Washington, D.C.

Petri, Peter. 1992a. "One Bloc, Two Blocs or None? Political-Economic Factors in Pacific Trade Policy." In Okuizumi, Kaoru, Kent E. Calder, and Gerrit W. Gong, eds., *The U.S.-Japan Economic Relationship in East and Southeast Asia: A Policy Framework for Asia-Pacific Economic Cooperation*. Significant Issues series, vol. 14, no. 1. Washington, D.C.: Center for Strategic and International Studies.

———. 1992b. "Platforms in the Pacific: The Trade Effects of Direct Investment in Thailand." *Journal of Asian Economics* 3(2):173–96.

———. 1993. "The East Asian Trading Bloc: An Analytical History." In Jeffrey A. Frankel and Miles Kahler, eds., *Regionalism and Rivalry: Japan and the United States in Pacific Asia*. Chicago: University of Chicago Press.

Ramstetter, Eric D., ed. 1991. *Direct Foreign Investment in Asia's Developing Economies and Structural Change in the Asia-Pacific Region*. Boulder, Colo.: Westview Press.

Rapp, William V. 1986. "Japan's Invisible Barriers to Trade." In Thomas A. Pugel, ed., with Robert G. Hawkins, *Fragile Interdependence: Economic Issues in U.S.-Japanese Trade and Investment*. Lexington, Mass.: Lexington Books.

Rivera-Batiz, Francisco L., and Luis A. Rivera-Batiz. 1990. "The Effects of Direct Foreign Investment in the Presence of Increasing Returns Due to Specialization." *Journal of Development Economics* (Netherlands) 34(Nov.):287–307.

Rodrik, Dani. 1993. *Trade and Industry Policy Reform in Developing Countries: A Review of Recent Theory and Evidence*. NBER Working Paper 4417. Cambridge, Mass.: National Bureau of Economic Research.

Safadi, Raed, and Alexander Yeats. 1993. "Asian Trade Barriers against Primary and Processed Commodities." Policy Research Working Paper 1174. World Bank, International Economics Department, Washington, D.C.

Salleh, Ismail Muhd, and Saha Dhevan Meyanathan. 1993. *Malaysia: Growth, Equity, and Structural Transformation*. Lessons of East Asia series. Washington, D.C.: World Bank.

Saxonhouse, Gary R. 1992. "Trading Blocs, Pacific Trade and Pricing Strategies of East Asia–Pacific Firms." Paper presented at the World Bank–CEPR Conference on New Dimensions in Regional Integration, April 2–3, World Bank, Washington, D.C.

Schott, Jeffrey J. 1991. "Trading Blocs and the World Trading System." *World Economy* (U.K.) 14(Mar.):1–17.

Stephensen, Sherry M. 1994. "ASEAN and the Multilateral Trading System." *Law and Policy in International Business* 25(2):439.

Takeuchi, Kenji. 1989. "Does Japan Import Less Than It Should? A Review of the Econometric Literature." *Asian Economic Journal* (Hong Kong) 3(Sept.):138–70.

Tokunaga, Shojiro. 1992. *Japan's Foreign Investment and Asian Economic Independence*. Tokyo: University of Tokyo Press.

UNCTAD (United Nations Conference on Trade and Development). 1983. *Non-tariff Barriers Affecting the Trade of Developing Countries and Transparency in World Trading Conditions: The Inventory of Non-tariff Barriers*. Geneva: United Nations.

———. 1993. *World Investment Report 1993: Transnational Corporations and Integrated International Production*. New York: United Nations.

United States. 1993. *Economic Report of the President to the U.S. Congress*. Washington, D.C.: Government Printing Office.

USITC (United States International Trade Commission). 1993. "Asia: Regional Economic Integration and Implications for the United States." Washington, D.C.

U.S. Trade Representative. 1993. "1993 National Trade Estimate on Foreign Trade Barriers." Office of the United States Trade Representative, Washington, D.C.

Whalley, John. 1992. "The Uruguay Round and the GATT: Whither the Global System?" University of Western Ontario, Canada.

Wolf, Martin. 1987. "Differential and More Favorable Treatment of Developing Countries and the International Trading System." *World Bank Economic Review* 1(4):647–68.

Wong, Kar-yiu. 1989. "Optimal Threat of Trade Restriction and Quid Pro Quo Foreign Investment." *Economics and Politics* 1(Nov.):277–300.

World Bank. 1992. *Global Economic Prospects and the Developing Countries*. Washington, D.C.

———. 1993a. *The East Asian Miracle: Economic Growth and Public Policy*. New York: Oxford University Press.

———. 1993b. "Viet Nam—Transition to the Market, An Economic Report." World Bank, East Asia and the Pacific Region, Country Department 1, Washington, D.C.

———. 1994a. *China: Foreign Trade Reform*. Washington, D.C.

———. 1994b. *Global Economic Prospects and the Developing Countries*. Washington, D.C.

———. 1994c. *World Development Report 1994: Infrastructure for Development*. New York: Oxford University Press.

Yeats, A. J. 1979. *Trade Barriers Facing Developing Countries*. London: Macmillan.

Young, Soogil. 1992. "Globalism and Regionalism: Complements or Competitors?" Korean Development Institute, Seoul.